All names mentioned in this book have either been asked permission or are of public figure status.

"First and foremost, apologies to all the English teachers out there. You are going to greatly dislike the grammatical choices made in this book." – Elijah Tindall

Thank you to all that allow me to do what I do and be who I am.

- God. For placing me on the earth for such a time as this. I wouldn't have done well in other seasons throughout history so sticking me in an airconditioned generation really means a lot.
- My wife, Stephanie. Your love, grace and support are the things I rely on daily. Thank you for being the blessing at the end of my broken road.
- My family, Destiny, Sheldon, Evan, Leila, Morgan and Ashton. You make me proud and I love you. Also, If I ever go on Family Feud, I am secretly hiring replacements because I want to win. But I still love you.

Preface –

This book is for the person who wants to grow. This is not everyone. It may sound weird but its true. Some people feel fine about where they are in terms of personal development while others feel they have already arrived. No more work to be done. I am not that person. My life is in constant need of growth. The moment I think I have attained wisdom in an area, something comes along and makes me feel the size I really am, small. I was once on an airplane at LAX (I won't say which airline, but I will say it was an American airline.). As we took our seats, the flight attendants in my section – a male who appeared to be in his mid to upper 40's and a female who feel in this same age category – were talking to each other pretty loudly. Not an angry dispute kind of loud, but more of a comfortable with each other type of conversation. A gentlemen one row up and across from me commented, "You guys must know each other pretty well". They looked at each other and almost simultaneously responded, "We've been working together for over 25 years". It caught my attention, so I decided to remove my giant headphones (which were plugged into nothing but it's a great way to get on a plane because you never know if the person sitting next to you is going to be a weirdo with horrible breath that wants to talk about strange things the whole time. This is a visual discourager of that. Also, why is it that people with bad breath always want to whisper secrets..?). As I removed the headphones I noticed that they started to brag about how they have seen other attendants come and go yet they are still there, on this, American airline. I shall not reveal which one. They continued to talk and boast about their time with the airline. It came across a little braggy but that was fine, people deserve moments to vent their accomplishments and if this was that for them, then so be it. The pilot was giving the usual pre-flight updates on weather conditions and flight times. They talked right over it. This is when I started to think they needed to take it down a notch. Not that the pilot was sharing vital information of danger, but just the fact that they were showing a disrespect toward another member of the crew, it just set the wrong way to me. 3 rows up and across from me, I noticed another pilot. He was dressed in full pilot attire and, I assume just catching a ride to the airport where he would fly out of. I could see the frustration building on his face as these two veterans of flight continued to brag and ignore. Meanwhile the plane was actively moving toward the runway. If you have ever flown out of a large airport, you know that this can take some time. Often there are planes in front of you and the line stacks up. I have sat for over an hour waiting to take off in the past, but not on this day. As the pilot told the crew, "Prepare for takeoff", these two Employees of the Month stood there in the isle and continued to discuss with the engaged passengers just how long they have been there. The look on their faces as the plane accelerated down the runway was a look of terror. They then realized what was happening. They were so comfortable with being people who know what to do because they have done it for so long, that they ignored the one they should have been listening to. They were operating out of familiarity. Their need to keep their ears open seemed miniscule since they were specialist in this field already. A 747 takes off at 180 miles per hour, and that is how fast these two were flying from the middle of the airplane to the back. They missed their window of opportunity to take their seats all because they assumed they didn't need to listen. They already knew…until the moment they realized they didn't. That is a very familiar position to be in. Maybe we have never flown through the air because of our pride, but we have all fallen because of it. The common denominator here is the pride to think we already know. This causes us to talk big, look foolish and hurt those we are supposed to be there to serve. As I watched these two take flight, I saw that the man was swinging his arms toward the seats in an attempt to stop himself and anchor. This unfortunately caused him to catch his watch on the upper arm of the elderly woman sitting beside me in the isle seat. Blood was flying everywhere. She screamed as his watch tore through her thin skin. I was trying to snap myself out of shock and into first responder mode, but I'm not gonna lie, it was hard. As a comic and communicator, I am always looking for material. And as a storytelling comic, I try to gather as much life experience observation as possible. This was Christmas for me. I forced myself to not immediately grab my notepad. I wanted to help, but what could I do? If these 2 Eagles of the industry lost their flight legs, I stood no chance (← impressive pun intended. It's why I make the big bucks). As all onlooking passengers did pretty much the same thing, reach their hands mid-way into the air as if they were the ones falling and sighed in a breath awaiting the landing of the stumbling attendants. Then, all at once and with honorable stage command, the transporting pilot from 3 rows up, stood from his seat. He was of noble decent, you could just see it in him. Complete with the thick Tom Sellick style mustache that I appreciate on a pilot, he balanced himself, turned into the isle and made his way to the fallen soldiers. Bracing himself with his left hand positioned on the top of a seat, he reached out with the right. Grasping the flailing forearm of the woman flight attendant, he pulled her upright and back on to her feet. He then made his way to the other. They held on to him like an anchor until the plane stopped its initial high-grade incline. They walked or limped to the back of the plane while the other flight attendant and heroic pilot tended to the bleeding woman sitting next to me. The hardest part of all of this was to watch these same flight attendants have to return to humility and do what they were there to do, serve people. Everyone they were boasting to and in front of now saw them fall. Not just fall but injure others in the process. What a humiliating position to be in.

I am concerned that too many people are in this same position of thinking. The assumption that they are above listening to others because they have been in the game longer and know more. It may be true that you know more but that doesn't matter in the moments when a team member is speaking concerning our current position and we ignore it. Pride always comes before a fall and my hope is that you take in the information being given in a way that prepares rather than repairs. I hope you are on the front end of the flight and not the floor of the plane. No matter where you may be, the information in this book will cause you to think, and if applied, grow. To some, it will be the pilot in the cockpit that is giving you instructional orders and to others, it may be the pilot in the seat here to help lift you from the fall. You are called to serve. If those you are called to serve are injured due to your lack of tuning in, it doesn't change the fact that you are still called to serve them. It will just be a little more humbling as you do so. You can be a person who humbles yourself, or you can let the pride and the plane do it for you. I ask you to be a person who says, "I need to grow". Because if so, this book is for you. If not, this book is still for you, you just won't know it until later. The good thing is, it will still be available wherever books are sold ☺

Chapter 1 - The Rockstar

I wasn't exactly sure how he could be drenched in sweat, yet his glorious flamboyant mane of hair never seemed to be affected by the moisture. I mean, I, personally spent at least 30 minutes every morning, blow-drying, crimping (yes crimping, it was 1986) and saturating my wavy locks in Aqua-Net, yet, for the life of me, could not keep the desired end-result. Each press of the spray cap released a layer of damp liquid concrete that would pass the equivalent of the motorcycle helmet law regulations in any of the great United States of America. The hydration of the product mixed with the humidity in the Arkansas summer air resulted in my hair becoming more Prince and the Revolution than Motley Crue. But not him, Nikki Sixx stood there a symbol of what things could be, if all the stars lined up for this 14 year-old Elijah Tindall. That was a unique time in my life. I wanted so bad to become a "Rockstar". There was a mix of emotions for this puberty ridden young man in that era. On one hand, my exposure to rap music had me freestyle battling other 8th graders on the parking lot of Mabelvale Jr. High in Little Rock, Arkansas, on the daily. While on the other hand, my exposure to early glam rock encouraged the growing desire to focus in on my drumming ability and pursue a future of colosseum tours and bright lights shining upon full body spandex suits. I was, at minimum, the most visually unique rapper in the parking lot. Skin-tight parachute pants, ripped up t-shirt, tall long hair, brushed in mustache (utilizing my mom's mascara) and Adidas shell toes. It was like a mash-up before mash-ups were a thing. My identity crisis didn't sway me from my dreams of success and those dreams eventually led me to the question we have all asked along the way…Why them? What is it that they are doing or have done that allows them to walk in the reality of the dream that I have on the inside. Is it talent? Is it a drive? Is it because of the money they started with? All these are very valid questions to explore, and when you get to the end of those, there will still be others. The truth is, all of us have different journeys that lead us to different stories. When it comes to pursuing our dreams, most of us spend more time picking apart the reasons other successful people "made it" than we do working to achieve realizing what is in our hearts. It seems to be so much easier to point out all the visible advantages they have and just stop there. I have found a truth along my path that applies to us all. No amount of critique towards others will ever equal the achievement of personal success. The more time I spend tearing down the hair advantages of Nikki Sixx, the less I will be open to learning from the foundational truths his story has to aid my journey toward successful hair, and more importantly, my ever becoming a "Rockstar".

Now, as those who are familiar with me know, I did not become a Rockstar. I do not play an instrument on stage in a large venue for a living. As a matter of fact, I haven't sat down and jammed with a group of other musicians in many years, but there was something about that part of my adolescent dreaming that did stick. I now find myself on stages at least 6 to 8 times a month. I do wear a lot of accessories, smudged eyeliner and still press my hair (flat iron now… no more crimping). My brand of hair spray has changed as the options broadened over the years. I spend the majority of my work life, encouraging others through comedy, motivational presentations and messages. I use a natural approach for me yet if you ask most onlookers, they would argue that my style is very different than what is usual or expected in most of the places I am invited. It isn't because I have a different finish line than the other speakers. It is only because my approach flows from a style that was developing inside me long ago. My desire to become a Rockstar as an adolescent exposed me to a larger dream for myself. That dream, as it were, allowed me to grow and began to shape the way I looked at things. That dream developed the way I saw myself. Over time, I realized that I could stand around complaining about the reasons other people became successful, or I could gather up my puzzle pieces and pursue my place in the history of this world's story. You too have a dream on the inside of you that is formative in the branding of who you are and what you hope to accomplish. We all do. Even if you are in the stage of life that seems uncertain about what your "dream" is or have yet to determine the exact career path for yourself, that doesn't change the fact that there is one. You are here on this earth for a very limited time and while you are here, you may as well live a life that makes a positive impact on others. And while you are at it, you may as well do so in a unique way that only you can do. It was never meant to be that we fit into a mold and only replicate the actions of others that came before us. We were all meant to do things with our own style in which we developed along the experience of our individual journey. The primary reason we must embrace this fact is because the sooner we do, the less time we will spend making excuses for ourselves by pointing at the advantages of others and the disadvantages we've been given. A victim mentality never produces a victor.

Yes, I wanted to be a Rockstar. No, I did not become one. BUT, had I never been exposed to the season of glam rock, with all its flamboyancy, I would have never become the flavor of communicator I am today. That dream was one of the ingredients in the recipe that made me who I am and who I am yet to become. Instead of me being upset that I never became the Rock legend I wanted to be and pointing at the advantages that Nikki Sixx was given, what with his glorious natural good hair and the fact that he lived in Hollywood California while I was being raised in the south. None of those factors equal me being a success. In fact, the harsh reality that hardly any of us want to embrace is that, even the people we declare have advantages, all operate in life with disadvantages that may not be visible to our eyes. We have a very limited vision when it comes to understanding other people's entire life experience. Just like in a poker game, or more applicable for my life, an UNO game. Each person has been dealt a hand that the rest of the players can't see. And let's just say that every card in their hand is a perfect set up, this does not mean that they will continue to be dealt perfect cards along the way. It could be that there will be seasons of hardship and unforeseen difficulty as time goes on. No one knows the whole story except the person who is living through it. You stay focused on you and not on what you wish you had that are in the hands of other people. The more you do that, the more you will find that others are looking at you in the exact same way. They are only wishing that they had some of the advantages you have been given. None of us have perfect stories and if everyone knew all the details we would all hide in embarrassment over the insecurities we feel due to the issues we've faced. So, let's all start on the same page right from the beginning of this book. No amount of criticism or judgment placed on others will ever equal forward movement when it comes to our success.

In the following chapters you will be handed information that will challenge your thinking. I may say a few things that will not be initially celebrated but I promise you this, if you will allow them to simmer for a while, they will expand your ability to clearly identify some of the things that have limited you on your journey to becoming the Rockstar you were meant to be. No, it may not ultimately look exactly how you thought it would at the start of your journey, but you will find that elements of each season will be the ingredients to the unique recipe that makes up the you that walks happily in the matured version of the dream you only thought you understood long ago. You will find the thing you used to see as the desired end-result was only a part of the bigger picture. As you go further, your dream becomes clearer. The limitations you were not aware of become visible and therefore, more avoidable. Thus, giving you forward motion in becoming the real you…not just the Rockstar you admired in someone else. Sure, you will take some of those experiences with you along the way, but they won't be the largest thing that defines you, because remember, the person you are wishing you were in the position of already exists, they already have their place, and even if you succeeded in your pursuit to become like them, at the end of that journey, there would be no need for you, because they have already filled that role. So more than anything, the world needs you to realize the dream of who you really are, and that, at its quickest will take our entire life to figure out. Before any of this can happen, we must first deal with invisible forcefield that seems to repel our dreams from coming to pass, our mindsets.

Chapter 2 – New You or Screw You?

Squinting to see past the stage lights that beamed through the haze and into the crowd, I did my best to stay in character while examining the room. It was a packed house, and there I stood, on stage, hunched over...in a muted green spandex body suit and bald cap. "How did I get myself into this?" is not a question I have asked very often, rather, "WHY did I get myself into this?" would be the more common thought. In my lifetime, I have been known to go All In without thinking it entirely through. That being said, this was not one of those moments. Weeks earlier, when I was in a creative meeting to discuss an upcoming church conference, I had no reservations at all about playing the role of Smeagol from Lord of the Rings. It would be in a spoof, 3 night skit called "Lord of the Offerings". Why would I?...more like why wouldn't I?! I mean, with award winning results, the 3rd movie had been released earlier in the year and my Smeagol impression was pretty spot on, if I do say so myself. As for the full body spandex suit, well, as an adult, at the awkward expense of those uncomfortable around me, I just have never been that shy of a person. Physical comedy is one of my favorite forms, and if the skinny, early 30's, chicken legged Elijah could get a few laughs wearing a spandex suit, then bring it on. If it was good enough for Poison, Quiet Riot and Mr. Goodbody, then it was good enough for me! The icing on the cake was that I loooooooved this character. *(From my first introduction to him – on screen, not in books. I'm sorry Hobbit fans, I was one of those people who jumped on the bandwagon when the movie came out. – a chord was struck.)* The bell of his internal, emotional battle for true identity rang so loud to me. Mainly because I believe he is a good representation of every person who has ever existed. For those who may not be familiar with him, let me give you a brief rundown of the premise. So, there was this guy named Smeagol who came across and took possession of this beautiful ring, and he became obsessed to say the least. Here's the kicker, this ring was forbidden, and just like all forbidden things that we hold on to, it began to destroy him. The ring itself belonged to the leader or lord of the darkness. The ring itself was trying to make its way back into the possession of this dark lord. It would draw its holder toward the dark to get closer to its goal. Therefore, due to the ring's influence, the holder/possessor would find themselves closer to darkness as they yielded to the power of the ring. Over time Smeagol's continence changed. His peace no longer prevailed and he found himself all alone, still holding onto and treasuring the one thing that was literally destroying him. This story is all too familiar, because I have seen it played out over and over throughout history. How many people do you know that have refused to let go of the things that literally cause destruction in their lives? No matter how much the facts stack up, for whatever reason, it is seemingly impossible to release. And the longer we hold on to our "ring", the worse we become. Whether it be an addiction, forbidden relationship, love of materialistic possessions, unforgiveness or anything else, when we embrace wrong things, they slowly chip away at the person we are truly meant to be on this earth. We don't have to look very far before we identify the thing/s we personally deal with that fall into this same "ring" category. But when in question, these things share the same characteristics. They all start with a sense of enticement. They all encourage secrecy. And they all demand more and more of us as we continue to allow them to be a part of our lives. Even though most of the time we are cautioned by others around us, we quickly go from the first stage of being tempted by it to eventually running with open arms, to it. In the mid and long term, it steals from us. And when it does, it hurts more than simply being robbed, because at least in a robbery, you don't have an emotional or physical attachment to the one robbing you. In this case, you do. You are committed to it. You have worked hard to attain it, keep it secret and maintain it. This, is why things become increasingly more difficult to walk away from. Because we have invested so much energy into their survival and as I have taught on many occasions, **sacrifice for attaches value to**. Any time we sacrifice parts of our energy and life into something, that thing becomes valuable to us. In addition to stealing from you, they also kill the healthy things the good part of your life grows. Just like a weed next to a plant in the soil, it will make its way over to the roots and begin to choke out growth. Always starting below the surface then gradually effecting the visible, outward produce. As you go along, you begin to wonder what ever happened to all the positive, peaceful things that were once a part of your life. The answer is, the weed has done its work, yet, for whatever reason, human nature is to continue to hide, protect and deny the fact that it is there. On top of that, we lash out at the ones close enough to us that point out the obvious deterioration. Their motive could be completely innocent and pure, but we are so committed to the ring, that we defend ourselves and its place in our lives.

Smeagol, in the story, eventually withers into a horrible version of himself named Gollum. Gollum's identity is a result of the presence of the ring (the thing that is destroying him). The part of the Movie that stuck with me the most is a dialog that he has with himself, Gollum to Smeagol. He literally changes countenance while talking as each character. One wanting to do good while the other wanting to continue to be the lowest version of himself. If that doesn't accurately describe us, I don't know what does. It seems that we all have the potential for two different versions of ourselves to show up at any moment. One is the version that we want to be, and the other is the version we hate. And even though we hate that version, we are very well aware that this lower form of us is the easiest one to conjure. It uses fleshly enticements as its muse. Surface level frustrations draw it to the surface. It wants to live and be in control at all moments. The problem is, this version of us destroys everything that the other version, the best version, builds. The two are easily identified by this, the good version acts and lives for the service of others, while the bad version acts and lives to serve self. There is the **New You** – The one that you are truly meant to be, and **The Screw You**, the one that is constantly screwing things up for you. If you are ever in question as to who you are being at any given time, just ask, "am I doing this for myself or others?". That question will usually expose our true motives.

In the Christian faith, an apostle named Paul, described his struggles in this area, in Romans 7:15. "For what I am doing, I do not understand. For what I will/want to do, that I do not practice; but what I hate, that I do." He clearly identified with the frustration of finding himself doing the exact things he stood against, while desiring to be a better person. Yet, all the stuff that he knew was right…the stuff he wanted to do, he did not do. Sounds like a crazy man to me, yet I know exactly what he is talking about here, because I have seen that same crazy man in the mirror on far too many occasions. I wish I could say that this sounded so foreign to me, but I can't. I too have been in positions where I sit and watch myself be the lowest form of who I could be in certain moments. The thing I want to do, I do not do, yet the thing I HATE, that is what I do. Paul goes on to say, in Romans 12:2, "Don't be conformed to this world, but be transformed by the renewing of your mind so you can prove what is the good, acceptable and **perfect will of God**". This indicates that God has a perfect will or plan already lined out for you. But, this perfect plan doesn't just happen, there is a process he lays out in this verse. Overall, conforming to this world will result in you walking in the "Screw You" identity, while transforming our minds will bring out the "New You" version that we really want to be.

Here is the Breakdown:

1. **Don't be conformed to this world** – Meaning, the product of allowing the things of "this world" to influence you will produce conformity in your life. "**Conformed**" *in terms of a person*, means to "Behave according to socially acceptable conventions or standards." At first, this doesn't sound so bad. I mean, overall, socially acceptable standards include general moral principles like, don't murder, don't steal, be a nice person and these types of things. Yet, though it may start on that level of standards, the problem is, the more we allow ourselves to compromise in areas, we find that we also allow our surroundings to decline. We gradually become more comfortable with things, places, conversations and people that live below the personal standard that we know as "right". As we adapt to this decline, our surroundings become more questionable. Therefore, you are now, based on the definition of "conformed", behaving according to socially acceptable conventions and standards of a lower level of living. What starts out as, not that bad, eventually gets worse and worse. Most of us are familiar with this lower standard version of ourselves. This version constantly screws things

up for you. That is why I call this version, The Screw You. He always screws you up. Conformity is the ever shifting backbone of The Screw You. This is NOT the version of you that you want in the driver's seat.

2. **Be transformed** – Meaning, changed. Much like a caterpillar does in the cocoon, transformation takes you from one form to another. The definition of "transformed", according to the dictionary, is, "make a dramatic change in form, appearance or character". So, according to this passage in Romans 12:2, The Apostle Paul is telling us to NOT be conformed to world around us, but rather to BE transformed (dramatically changed in form, appearance or character). The question is, how? How do we resist the conformity and begin the transformation? And more importantly, for those of you who think like me and aren't willing to immediately do something just because someone says so (seeking clarity and understanding first are not bad things), the bigger question is, WHY? What's so wrong with just letting things play out and see how we end up? Let's go on in the breakdown of this scripture and I believe the "how" and "why" will be addressed to our satisfaction.

3. **By the renewing of your mind** – The implication here is, transformation is to be attained by "renewing our mind". I can see, at minimum, a 2-part process in this step.

A. Our minds must be changed – certain ways of thinking that we have embraced along the way must change. This proves to become difficult on a personal level because, though we readily identify wrong ways of thinking in others, we rarely consider that we also are wrong. As a matter of fact, statistically speaking, the majority of people that just read that last sentence desire to put this book down now. Merely the suggestion that we are wrong causes us to shut down. But it doesn't take much to reveal that we have been wrong before, just think back on your life. Take a few of those "If I had it to do over" moments and consider that you were wrong then. Yet, if we would've suggested to you back then that you were wrong, most likely we would find the same defensive response. We do not like to be told we are wrong. It's just human nature, we defend the ring. A teenager will argue with grown, life seasoned adults till they are exhausted over points that we know to be simple. We see how foolish it looks when they do it, yet, we proudly carry that same, pride filled spirit with us into adulthood and do the same thing. Just like with addiction therapy, we must first admit there is a problem. And, just like with an addict, most of us don't want to do that. In doing so, we acknowledge that we have allowed ourselves to embrace a limitation and possibly even an untruth and live by its standard. This is why it is so hard to grow into the larger, better version of ourselves. Because the younger, **know it all** version has never let go of the wheel. We must first admit, we do not know everything. That is the easier of the two, because we point to obvious things like Rocket Science and say, "I'm no Rocket Scientist"or "You can't expect me to know everything". But it's harder to point to things within our everyday life and say "I don't know". After that, the even harder part is opening ourselves up to admitting that some of the things we thought we knew, may be wrong. This leads me to the second part of the process,

B. Embracing new thoughts. Have you ever thought you knew the right lyrics to a song? You sang it loudly and proudly. Then, one day, there was something that happened that showed you the correct lyrics. Most of the time this happens in a public setting, to assure the most humiliation possible. Those few moments when your mind fights for the old lyrics are hilarious. You go though a process of thinking/saying, "no"…then you say what you thought it was out loud while you justify how it made sense. Eventually, you take on the new found lyrics and forevermore, your mindset is changed concerning that song. Why, because you have been exposed to the right set of words. This, in Christian terms is called "Revelation knowledge". A revelation is not just the name of the last book in the Bible. My simple definition for revelation knowledge is this: *Having a greater understanding of something you thought you knew in the first place.* Just like in the case of the wrong lyrics, you thought you knew the true words the whole time. Yet, at some point, you were confronted with an opposing truth. That truth was larger than the original one you embraced before. You went from thinking you knew, to knowing. This is how growth works. But, the reason most stop the growing process in their own lives is because of pride. Pride refuses to admit there are things we could be wrong about. It rejects new thoughts that conflict with current understanding. For those that are open to transformation based on renewing of the mind, we must allow ourselves to be introduced to new thoughts. New thoughts come from new exposure. We must be **exposed to** new things in order to be **presented with** new things. Example, most men, in most places of the world are in the practice of wearing pants. Almost everywhere the eye gazes, men in pants. This seems like a foolish fact to bring up in the context of our current culture. Especially where I live, here in the United States. It does not seem to stretch the mindsets of the average person to openly declare, pants are okay. Yet, believe or not, there was a time when one would have no idea what you were describing if you dared to say something like, "let me throw on a pair of pants, real quick.". As far as we have traced, pants were introduced between the 13th and 10th century, BC. They were created for people who rode horses on long distance journeys in the Western China area of the world. Can you imagine never, EVER having seen a pair of pants and there you are, lounging about in your robe like usual, when, all of a sudden, a rider strolls up in a pair of…pants! I am sure that there were tons of resistance from those not willing to embrace this new style. I mean, even Jesus wore a robe. How could we dare think that this is okay? The fact is, as most all of us have concluded, pants were actually a good thing. Just because we do not initially understand something does not mean it is to be completely disregarded. Yet that seems to be our response with most things when it comes to a challenge to the way we think…because I do not understand it to be right or true, must mean it is wrong or false. That is such a small way to live. We must be willing to at least be exposed to the pants before we just say they are rubbish. How many things have you written off along the journey of your life that may have been an additive? It is impossible to say from the perspective of one who has never tried. It is as simple as this, what you believe and think right now is a direct result of something you were exposed to in your past. Had you not been exposed to it, you would have never embraced it. If that is true, and it is, then why are we not living life everyday with a sense of pursuit of new things? Why are we not initiating new friendships with people that are different than us? Exposure equals potential growth. I say "potential" because not everything or everyone is going to cause us to grow, but NO ONE and NOTHING will certainly cause us to stay the same. In my opinion, its worth the risk. While speaking in a leadership panel to young people between the ages of 13 to 24, we were asked the question, "How do I find what my gifting is?". That is a big question in which I had a very simple answer, "TRY EVERYTHING. As much as you can find opportunity to do, do it." (Obviously, within the boundaries of safety and morality). While trying **everything**, you will find the **something**. Not only will you find the something, you will also find the some**things.** You will go from having no potential direction to having multiple options that build upon each other. But the key is to place yourself in positions you have never been in before. Resist the excuses that act as speed bumps on your path. Excuses like, "I'm just not good at things like that". Not being good at something is a very poor reason to keep from trying it. I have found that most often, we are not good at things we don't practice. Sure, we hear about those prodigies that immediately have amazing natural talent the moment they try something. But even in those cases, they have to try it. Things will not just reveal themselves when it comes to growth. They will slowly develop over time in their specific environments. This means, most of the time, we have to go to them – to their environment- not wait for them to come to us. If we do not take the step toward new things and expose ourselves to their environment, we will see them as a threat when they eventually enter our environment. Our mind set (the way our mind is set) will not be ready for the newness of the concept of things like "pants" and we will spend our time and effort leading oppositions that are pointless. Sure, some things are not to be embraced, but just because there are **some** things doesn't mean that **all** things are to be resisted. This is where we count on the inward witness of the Holy Spirit to lead us into all truth. If we carry the presence of God with us, and He is the ultimate truth, then why are we afraid of finding ourselves in the presence of untruth? We literally carry truth with us. This means, when we do come across things that we should not think like or embrace, the truth directs us, leads us and counsels us inwardly. I get pretty worn out listening to fear based thinkers who try to discourage people from trying new things and being open to different thoughts. Mindsets expand much like the physical body grows. As we use our muscles in certain ways, we find that they slowly develop and eventually the results can be seen outwardly. Beyond that, when we do something that demands different motion, those same muscles that we considered to be developed, become sore. The reason is because we exposed them to new movement. Exposure to "new" always carries the potential for growth. Much like the way we desire to be "right" when it comes to our mindsets, we are also very defensive about defending our physical health shortcomings. The difference is, when it comes to physical health, it is not hard to find ourselves in the midst of others that are beyond us. They are all around. We see them at the store where we shop. We see them at the restaurants we frequent. Everywhere we go, there is a good potential to see people that operate in good habits physically. Therefore, it's easier to identify and admit, we need work. In the case of the mind, until someone express outwardly, it is more difficult to identify how others are thinking. Sure, there are indicators. Style of clothing, choice of haircuts, physical characteristics of spouse...these all point toward preferences. Preferences are most certainly indicators of mindsets but most of these are very surface level. They rarely make a huge statement socially. The true test to find how someone thinks is to let them talk. "From the abundance of the heart, the mouth speaks". So, what your heart is full of, eventually makes its way out of your mouth. You fill your heart up with your thought life. Mind filters to heart, heart filters to mouth (or social media posts, as it were). It becomes a cycle very quickly. We are initially exposed to a mindset, we embrace that mindset as complete truth, we find people who believe the same way. Our lives start to box in to a tribal way of living. We find stations on the television who think and talk the same way as we have been exposed to, and we only watch them as our source of information. There is nothing wrong with owning certain ways of thinking, there is, however, something wrong with the assumption that one couldn't expand beyond that. I always tell people to "add to who you are but don't change who you are". We must stop this prideful position we have taken and admit that there is more to be experienced. More to be explored and more to be learned. This will only happen by being exposed to "new/different". But here we sit, surrounded by people who look like us, talk like us, act like us and we tend to resist others who come along that have another perspective. Being **transformed** by the **renewing** of our mind isn't going to happen by assuming our mindsets are already complete. And if it doesn't happen, then we will not find God's perfect plan for us.

4. So you may prove, what is God's perfect will. When I was 15, I sat in the back seat of the school bus. It was my first day taking this bus and I just preferred to sit in the back. There is less chance of getting spit-wads straw blown into the back of your hair if no one sat behind you, and I had long hair. Maybe that is the reason, who knows. Nevertheless, there I sat. I was completely taken by surprise when a 9th grader, complete with mullet and dangling cross earing walked on the bus with a group of friends and said, "You're in my seat.". I quickly evaluated the situation and, in classic jr. high form, responded, "I don't see your name on it". These were fighting words and we all knew it. Truth was, I didn't want trouble. This guy was way bigger than me and even worse, he had a bunch of friends to impress. I hardly knew anyone and those that I did know didn't ride my bus. Surrounded by the smell of Polo cologne mixed with cigarette smoke, I sat alone. He informed me that if I didn't move, he would kick my butt…only he didn't say "butt". I knew something was about to go down and I had to either swallow my pride, use wisdom and move, or stand up to his reign of terror in the hind quarters of the bus. So, being 15, I ignored wisdom, stood up and said, "prove it". At this point I would like to say that a fight broke out and I won, but nay. Well, actually, the first part was correct. A fight did break out. But I did not win. When I said, "prove it", turns out, he backed up his promise to kick my butt. A declaration was verbally made, and action was taken that proved out what he declared. I now think about that experience every time I hear the word, **prove**. This scripture states that God has a perfect will/plan for us and that, much like the 9th grader in the back of that bus, He is willing and able to prove it. When we don't allow ourselves to submit to His will, it puts satan in the place of authority in our lives. That is God's position. It's His throne. When He sees the devil seated on his throne, He is ready and willing to remove Him, but it is up to us to allow that to happen. We must resist the temptation to stay the same. He wants us to go through the process of transforming our minds so that He can prove His perfect will in our lives. It is only through His perfect plan that we walk in our true identity…**The New You**.

The New You verses The Screw You is written to help us identify the difference between the two and lean each reader toward God's perfect plan for their lives. Since finding that plan is a matter of transforming our minds, I will lead you through a series of 5 mindsets that have proven to hold people back. Five mindsets of limitation. I call these mindsets, Crazy Thoughts. Spoiler alert, the word CRAZY stands for Can't, Rejection, Attitude, Zeal and Yesterday. We will look at each one and how they affect our thought life. This will be a fun, but challenging journey. As you read, I encourage you to get a note pad and jot down areas of your own life that you see any of these CRAZY thoughts. Once identified, they can become targets to shot rather than weights to carry. My goal is to help lead you toward The New You because, let's be honest, The Screw You has been in the driver's seat for far too long when it comes to a few areas in your life. If not, you most likely wouldn't have purchased this book. So, let's not let all those dollars go to waste, let's get this thing started!

BONUS TRACK:

As evidence that mindsets can be misguided, I am interjecting a current list of the top 10 fears people deal with here in the United States. This is something I like to look up on a yearly basis because it is a good indicator of where we are, mentally, as a people. Before you look at these, I want you to think about what you would put on a fear list. Once you do, read this list. As you do, I think you may find it as surprising and amusing as me. And don't you worry about its accuracy, I gathered it from the internet so we can assure its validity. If you are one of those people who like to just read books for the points, feel free to skip straight to Chapter 3. For the rest of us, we are going to enjoy a look and thoughts on this list. After all, life is too short to not enjoy poking fun at ourselves.

Top 10 Fears

10. Death

Let me remind you of how a top 10 list works. 10 is the furthest away from 1. Meaning that people have literally said to themselves, "I would rather DIE than have one of the next 9 things take place". Look, those of you reading that are Christian like me may be telling yourself that you aren't afraid to die. I get that. I also understand that the Apostle Paul said, "absent in the body, present with the Lord." I know I know, we aren't afraid to die, but none of us want to die now! I have been on my death bed with 98% blockage in my heart while awaiting a quadruple bypass and I can tell you. I was not thinking, there are probably 9 things worse than this. I ain't tryn to die. But, if I should go sooner than my loved ones, I want to make it clear as to my expectations. 1. I want "I've seen a million faces and I rocked them all" written on my grave stone. And 2, embalm me with a terrified look on my face and hands in an upright, guarded position as if I am about to be hit by a bus. I request this juuuuuust in case I have the ability to watch the funeral in spirit form. I would love to see the look on my friends faces as they step up to the casket, look in and see me like this. I would just laugh and laugh...unless my passing is actually from being hit by a bus. In that case disregard what I just said. The main reason I thought Death being number 10 was so interested is because of the thing one time worse on this list, Number 9. (And I hesitate to even include this next one but the internet leaves me no choice. Just know I am classier than this...way stinkn classier.)

9. Vomiting

Yes, you read that correctly. Vomiting is on the TOP 10 fears list. One time worse than death. I get it, no one likes being sick, but worse than dying? I have never been in the bathroom sick and moaned, "I would rather die than this". Never. It is a horrible experience for sure. We do that motion like God is plunging us up by the back with an invisible plunger. The watery sensation and the moment we realize just how much cleaning still needs to be done around and inside the toilet bowl. But number 9? That seems a bit extreme. Out of all the things going on in todays society, I can't imagine a person over the age of 7 who would literally put this on their list. Nevertheless, it is there.

8. Thunderstorms

Being a person who grew up in the south, born in Dallas, raised in Little Rock and spent 12 years in Oklahoma City thereafter, I can tell you, there is no way this survey was conducted in that part of the country. People in the middle and East Coast of the U.S. all know what it's like to experience tornadoes. Once you have hunkered down with your family in a hallway closet, thunderstorms just don't make the cut as a top 10 fear. For us, hearing the newscaster say "severe thunderstorm warning" means absolutely nothing. We don't get off the couch until we see the red dot on top of our neighborhood on the little transparent state map in the lower corner of our screen. You can always tell when someone is from a tornadic region because they all do the same thing upon hearing the warning siren, we go to the front porch. As if we are completely exempt from being affected by high pressure winds and baseball sized hail. We just walk out there and look up. Once we see the circular clouds dipping down like evil fingers out of the sky, we then call our spouse out to the porch to see. Admittedly, something isn't quite right with our heads. None of it makes a lot of sense, including the instructions weather reporters give our children. "Children, if you are home alone and you can hear this, here is what we would like you to do. Go into the restroom in the middle of your home. Get into the bathtub in the restroom in the middle of your house…and place a mattress on top of you." Let me ask you a question. What child can carry a MATRESS?!? I am a full-grown man, my blood-sugar would be so low by the time I navigate those hallway turns. The difficulty of moving mattress' is the reason I refuse to move. The point is, we do not think of thunderstorms as a giant threat. Especially not one that is 2 times worse than death.

7 – Cancer

Weird for me to get excited about cancer showing up on any list, but in this case, I needed something of validity to be present, and here it is. There is nothing amusing about this subject for me to have comedic commentary OTHER than the fact that it is less concerning to Americans than number 6 on the list, Fear of Wide Open Spaces.

6 – Wide Open Spaces

I have flown over the majority of the United States and conclude that most of it is, in fact, nothing but a wide-open space. So, when I saw this on the list, it surprised me a bit. I can't help but to think that if this places sixth on the list, there must be a ton of folks trembling right now. It is not healthy to criticize phobias we do not suffer from, but honestly, I don't even know how you find that you have this one. I guess perhaps as you are walking one day, you hear a thunderstorm a brewing, want to vomit and say to yourself, "I would rather die than all of this". I think the only fear I've ever had in a wide-open space was the fear that someone was going to throw me the ball. Like I instructed in my last book, if you are like me and not good at sports, the key to getting through is to never make eye contact with the person who is holding the ball. Other than that, I usually feel pretty secure in a wide open field. But clearly there are those of you out there that disagree.

5 – Small Closed Spaces
This is one I have heard of. No one likes the thought of being locked in a car trunk. But if you are, here is a piece of very valuable information. Law now requires all trunks to be equip with an emergency pull chord to open the trunk from the inside. 2 things. 1, Great! 2, how many people were getting locked in trunks that the federal government had to get involved? I am sure the mafia is still alive and well but this, to my understanding was an old-school way of transporting the threatened store owner when refusing to pay his share for protection in the neighborhood. Haven't we advanced in society? I thought threats were mainly delivered via text now, I guess not. Word of advice, just pay the money. If not, I think the fear of small closed spaces is being misplaced with the fear of wearing concrete shoes and sleeping with the fishes. No, wait. That is fear number 10 on the list. My bad.

4 – Flying
Now we are talking! I dealt with this fear my entire early life. It wasn't until I turned 21 that I actually took my first flight. I. Was. Terrified. It was from Little Rock, Arkansas to Dallas, Texas. Less than 45 minutes. 45 minutes of pure terror that is. If you don't believe in speaking in tongues you would by the time you got off that flight. Each tiny bit of turbulence was met by a gasp for air and a loud moan by the 6 foot 1 inch, Hispanic

man in seat 13B, me. Over time, I learned a few things about airplanes and airport culture, mainly, I learned that they are on a mission to scare you. I think it's just their way of having fun at the job. If you don't believe me, let me ask you a question as I point a couple of things out. Why in the world, would we ever name anything at the airport, TERMINAL? Answer: Messing with us. Also, Why when approaching landing does the flight attendant say, "We are making our FINAL descent".? I am not comfortable with that terminology at all. If you need more to chew on, how about this. Have you ever noticed that about 30 minutes after you get up to cruising altitude, the entire place drops about 3 feet. It scares every one except the flight attendants. Why, because they know that its just the pilot playing with the big controller thing there in the cockpit. It is their way to watch us all do the same exact thing. We grab the seat handles and dare not move a muscle. We tense up to the point where we don't even turn our heads to look out the window. We only use our eyes. Firstly, why are we all grabbing those seat handles? It is like we are all thinking to ourselves, "pull up, PULL UP". It isn't going to help. Then, after that, the bumps will happen 2 more times. The second time, an arrogant male passenger nearby will make eye contact with the first person he can and say the following, "It's okay. I fly all the time". His non-chuluant mannerism will indicate he is relaxed. As if him flying all the time will help us in a potential dangerous situation. Finally, on the third large bump, emerges the evidence that they really are only messing with us. There is a vague, faint sound indicating the intercom came on. If you listen really closely, you can hear the distant sounds of the pilot talking. And when I say talking, I mean mumbling. This person's words are impossible to understand. The volume seems so low but we know the system works because we just sat through the schpill the flight attendants put us through before take-off. "If you are seated in an exit isle and are unable or unwilling to help in the case of an emergency".. Wait. I can understand unable, but who is unwilling!? You are telling me the plane goes down and somehow we are all still alive. Only one thing left to do, exit the plane. We make our way through the smoke, get to the exit isle and are met with an arm-folded man shaking his head no. "I am unwilling", he declares. It doesn't make sense. (Back to the shy pilot) The only thing we can seem to make out are the words, "We are experiencing a little, choppy air". Choppy air. That is the explanation for all this bouncing around, choppy air. To the unaware, this sounds like it must be accurate, but not me. Remember, I lived in Oklahoma City, AKA tornado alley for 12 years. If anyone knows about air fluctuation change, its certainly the people in these regions. In all my years of living among the treacherous winds, I have never seen anyone walking around outside and just drop to the ground. Wipe the dirt off their pants and reply, "Choppy air out here today!"

3 - Heights
I conclude that it is not as much the height that bothers people as the potential of falling from it. Specifically, from the plane mentioned in the last point. "We are making our final descent".

2 – Speaking in Public

This is one that I used to struggle with when I was younger and apparently, I was not alone. Over half of the population of the world is mortified to talk in front of a group. Now that I am on the other side of this fear, I can say that some of the advice I have heard is absurd. Like, just pretend everyone in the audience is naked…excuse me? Who was the first person to say this and what kind of meeting was this? If I am nervous already, I can't imagine how a group of naked people would do to calm my nerves. No thanks. Also, as social media has proven, this fear is much different than the fear of being SEEN in public. It seems that everyone wants to be seen. I think the key here is this. To speak in public means we must have something to say, and, well, lets just be honest. Most people don't. It's the image of depth that most go for. It is much easier to look like a valuable person than to actually bring value by speaking in public.

1 – Fear of Spiders

Yes, for the 10th year in a row, the fear of spiders tops the list. Let me remind you, this is, at least on the survey, considered to be 9 times worse than dying. Don't get me wrong, I hate the sight of a spider. I am not trying to prove how tough I am. For lord's sake, I wear eyeliner. I'm not the vision on manliness, but I don't agree that its worse than dying. Here is how much I don't like spiders. If ever I was on one of those survival shows and they said to me, "for $50,000, eat this spider.", I would just work harder. I am NOT eating a spider. In fact, to let you know how much I hate spiders, I will share this personal story with you before I conclude the Bonus Track and get into Chapter 3. Years ago, when my son, Evan was about 3 years old, my daughter, Destiny and I, were folding clothes in the living room. We heard a sudden scream from the other side of the house. I could tell it was a fear based scream so I starting running through the house like the hero I was meant to be. "Daddy, Daddy, theiw (he didn't have his R's down yet" is a spidew in hewe!". I immediately pressed the breaks and stopped in the dining room. I walked back to the living room and told Destiny, "your brother is calling you in the kitchen". There, I said it. I am not proud of it, but at least its out there. I can now wipe my hands clean of it. I. Hate. Spiders. Yet, as much disdain I hold told these demonic beings, I still hold that they are not 9 times worse than dying!

Chapter 3 – CAN'T

Can't is a CRAZY thought.

Bumble-bees can't fly! Well, let me rephrase that, it is impossible for Bumble-bees to fly. Sounds weird doesn't it. The fact that we have all seen a Bumble-bee fly far too close in proximity to our faces at one time or another causes us to know that this statement is faulty. Yet, according to Aviation standards, there is no possible way to recreate a flying object using the same dimensions as a Bumble-bees body. You see, it's little bitty wings are too small to carry the large torso and fuselage. The only one who doesn't know all this information is the Bumble-bee. That little joker just seems to wake up every day, put on its striped suit (of which, it is so confident, that even though it is thick, it wears its stripes horizontal.) and flies. Not only does it impossibly carry its own wait on these wings, because of its size, the bumble-bee is actually the highest producer when it comes to pollination. So, in case you aren't keeping count, that is now 2 things that the bumble-bee is doing far beyond what we have established to be within the realms of possibility. Like I have said before, we want to think that we are right/correct. We have facts, we have educated answers based on scientific research, yet here we are, being buzzed by every day. I believe that each and every one of us have been given "wings" of some sort. They may not be the thing that others look at and say, "Now THAT is the reason they will be successful". For some of us, it is actually the reason people say we will not be successful in certain areas. I know that was the case for me. When I was a child, I had a horrific stuttering issue. I couldn't reach the end of a sentence to save my life. I just stood there trying to avoid conversation. My issue was so problematic that even my 5th grade teacher said to me, "Elijah, I don't know what it is that you will end up doing when you are a grown-up, but whatever it is, it sure won't be talking". Hmmmm, yet for over 28 years now, I have literally talked for a living. She wasn't trying to be mean. She was simply doing what most of us do, pointing out the size of the wings. This could even be considered helping point someone in the right direction. Yet, much like the Bumble-bee, I was meant to flap. I am convinced that we are surrounded with potential that we look at as limitation. We look at the facts as truth. Facts declare that our task is big and our wings are small, therefore we must be focused on the wrong task. FACT: As an adolescent, I stuttered. It is not an un-truth, but it is not the ultimate truth. TRUTH: I was destined to speak for a living at a high level to millions around the world. Truth declares that we have been given large tasks to develop us into stronger beings and, even more importantly, to highlight the God that chooses to give limited people the strength to accomplish impossible things. We must give the facts time to develop into the truth. Never make permanent determinations based on temporary situations. Fact, you may not be able to pay your light bill at this moment. Truth, the light bill will eventually get paid. Fact should not be the enemy of truth, it is only the introduction to a great story of overcoming. If you ask me, the Chicken needs to be scheduling an appointment with the Bumble-bee. Maybe get a few pointers. I mean, think about it, out of the two, doesn't it seem as if the chicken should be the one to have the ability to fly? Yet, nothing. The chicken just spends its days plucking around until it gets picked up, brutally killed and then slaughtered, put on a plate and served up. That sounds so much like us in areas of life doesn't it. Instead of flying and soaring out of the attack, we are daily just plucking around, getting slaughtered and served up. I've yet to go into one restaurant and seen a Bumble-bee platter. Yet every eatery in the world contains a chicken option of some sort. Why is this, because the bumble-bee soars away while the chicken plucks around. Stop plucking around friend. It is time to soar. Stop looking at the wings you've been given as not enough. The task that is in front of you may look impossible, but the capacity inside of you is well able. You just have to change your mindset from CAN'T to CAN.

Philippians 4:13 says, "I CAN do all things through Christ which strengthens me". This is a scripture that most believers in Christ have heard and quoted many times. Its declaration is that we have been given the CAN ability. Yet, despite the information, most of us (Christians), live with just as much of a CAN'T mentality as the rest of the world. I think this to be a result of ministers who have taken this scripture out of context and used it as a way to just declare whatever it is you want to have or do, you only have to speak it out and believe it. Other religions and beliefs include this mentality as well. This is NOT what I am saying in this chapter. I believe that each person was created here with a specific task or assignment. It is for that assignment that we have been given the wings. The bumble-bee may be defying impossible things by flying and carrying more pollen than all other bees but it is not being used to carry people from state to state as an airline. That is not what it is created to do. So, no matter how much the Bumble-bee confesses and proclaims "I can do all things through Christ who strengthens me", he will not be able to do a task outside of what he is created for. While the principle of "Speaking things that are not as though they were", is real. We must balance it with God's perfect will as talked about in Romans 12:2. I can declare and ask God for a YES till I'm blue in the face but if it is outside of His plan, He will not honor the request. Some are thinking about the scripture reference "God's promises are yes and amen". I completely agree with that reference because it begins with "God's promises". If the thing we are asking God for is not one of His promises than we just may get a no. We have to be okay with that. The key in this passage is "through Christ which strengthens me". What does Christ strengthen me to do? What he designed me to do. Outside of that, we are subject to our own abilities. For instance, I can shout that scripture at the top of my voice from a 4-story building and believe I have the power to fly (literal, not Bumble-bee analogy like we've been talking..you get it). Once I step off the edge of the rooftop, the law of gravity will take over and I will go splat. It is not a matter of faith, it is a matter of location. Is my faith in the location of my call and design? My wings are for speaking, yours may be for hearing (counselor), art, parenting, pastoring, teaching, so many different areas that are each unique. There wouldn't be room enough to list out all the possibilities even if I tried. The key here is to look for the potential tasks then meet them with a I CAN rather than I CAN'T response. It is a matter of changing a CAN'T mentality into a I CAN at (at least try) mentality. Mindsets are stubborn and take time to grow out of and even once we have caught a glimpse of CAN, it is hard to hold on to. We must continually exercise CAN just like a muscle in order for it to be established as a mindset.

Speaking of muscle, I have a workout story that applies (master segue).

Get BIG

I once wanted to get big. Now when I say that, I don't mean big as in larger than I was, I mean from David Banner into the HULK "big". I was 19 years old and thin as the stretched-out cowboy on the old movies that they wouldn't convert to tv format back in the 80s, so it squished the sides in to make everyone super thin and tall. I tried everything to gain weight. I ate straight peanut butter with a spoon during the days. I'm not talking about the health food store peanut butter either. Straight up JIFF or Skippy by the cupful. It didn't budge the scale. – For reference, I think it's important to convey that I have since reached my forties and no longer struggle with this issue. I gain weight by simply looking at pictures of food now. My as have turned into AB. One big one right in the middle. I feel like a potato with toothpicks for legs and arms. But not back then. Back in those days, my 165-pound body refused to take on any sort of fat or muscle. I looked like a patient of some sort that escaped. In my effort to start the process of growing in muscle mass, I recruited the help of three body builders that I happened to know. They, amusingly said yes. I, knew even at that age and state of malnutrition that if you want to get bigger, you get around bigger people. This is a principle of life in all areas. If you are broke financially on a regular basis, it helps to rub shoulders with a few people that are constantly in a place of wealth and prosperity. Not so they can see you have need and pay your bills, nay. But so that their way of thinking and operating begins to rub off on you. In the right case, you may even want to ask them, if you had what I had, and wanted to grow it into what you have, where would you start? This allows us to see the difference in our thinking verses theirs. We often just say, "Well if I had what THEY have, it would be easy". But it could be that if we did have what they have, we would not be able to retain it due to our inability to manage things on that level. Asking questions helps us to know where we are off base in terms of leading, managing and retaining. In situations like this, we spend too much time wanting to defend ourselves with excuses and never listen or watch to see the difference in how they do it verses how we do. And, for the sake of saying the same thing you have read and heard over and over, if you always do what you've always done, you will always have what you've always had. Same goes with relational issues. If you want a great marriage, get around a loving couple. Want good dance moves, get around a dance class where they don't just watch videos but they actually learn the moves. My dance class, in this story, was the gym. I was ready to grow! I remember it so well, chest day. Now, for those of you who are unaware, chest day may as well be titled Man Day at the gym. There is just something about it that reeks of testosterone. Maybe it's due to the fact that as you do exercises like bench press, while targeting your pectoral muscles, it also sends the blood rushing through your tri-ceps as well as giving your upper shoulders and traps a good pump. No matter how small you may be, after a good set on the bench, you felt a little more of a man. No male that works out hates chest day. Leg day, that is a whole different story. We skip leg day with consistency, but not chest day. It. Was. Chest. Day. Toward the middle of our work out, we changed from an incline bench to a straight bench press type machine. It wasn't a free weight bench, it was more of a nautilus type machine that you put free weight on. We decided that the 3 body builders would go first then I would go last wrapping up each set. Our system was to put on the weight, lift it 10 times on the first set. The second set we would add weight, lift it 8 times and lastly, the third set, put on the max amount of weight and attempt to lift it 6 times. This was a system for stretching, tearing and growing the muscle…in that order. When trying to grow, you must be stretched to the point wear it damages a little bit of the old you. Remember the term growing pains? This is where it came from. In order to have growth, you must have change. It is possible to change without growing but it is impossible to grow without changing. Growth requires change and change can hurt. But, this is what I was there to do, grow. The first of the three sets began. The first guy put his weight on. Three 45-pound plates on each side. I am not sure how much weight that actually is, no one knows, but it is a lot. Then, he sat on the bench, grunted and lifted the weights 10 times. It was like a room full of silverback gorillas and one chimpanzee. We were very excited. The next barbarian got on and did the same feat, as did the following. Then came my turn. At that point, the workout came to a slight pause due to the fact that we needed to swap out the weights. They all were lifting the same amount, three 45-pound plates on each side. Once again, no one knows how much that amount comes to. They removed their weight. Each plate scraping the weight bar causing a vibration that amounted in the sound of deep, southern thunder. After all, 6 plates were removed, on came my weights. 15 pounds on each side. A 10 (cling), and a 5 (clang). While their plates equaled a thunderous sound, mine was more like an empty aluminum can being thrown into a well-padded trash can. I wasn't discouraged though. Not one bit. Sure, in the past I had lifted more weight than I was at this moment. But this was the first time I was under the tutelage of others who actually knew how to produce the results I was aiming for. Off I went, lifting my heart out. Though it wasn't very much weight, it did cause me to struggle a bit due to me keeping correct form and not just throwing it up all sloppy like. 10! I completed the first set. The next set consisted of the guys putting their weights back on and adding additional weight, then lifting said weight 8 times. My set came, off came theirs and on came mine, 20 on each side. I was increasing and I could feel it. Finally, on the 3rd and last set, as we were in a serious and deep conversation (what about? Glad you asked. The conversation was on the topic of back hair removal. I learned that day that no matter who big and defined you are, in a body building competition, people DO NOT vote for the fuzzy one. They, for whatever reason want you to be slick, tan and greased up.), the Viking right in front of me in the lineup received a phone call. Now this was back in the days before we all carried the universe in our pockets. Back then, phones were on a thing called chords. He, told me, "You do your set now in my place and I will come back and finish my set after you". I, being of sound mind and not wanting any physical harm, gladly agreed. I sat down and started pressing. The weight was heavy. I lifted with all of my might. This was the max out set so it was supposed to be harder than the rest and if you remember, we were only trying to lift these 6 times. After a very hard press, I completed the task. King Kong returned from his phone call and we went to adjust the weight to let him have his last set. That is when it happened… We realized that we were so ingulfed with this conversation on back hair removal, that we forgot to ever take his weight off. That means me, Sméagol, just lifted HIS weight! Something happened to me that day… (low, deep, raspy voice) I became a man that day. I immediately did what every other guy reading this would do. I told the guys, "Let me lift this one more time!". They, being dumbfounded, agreed. I sat down and counted off the before lift. "ONE….TWO…..THREE". And as I pushed as hard as I could, nothing happened. The weight just stayed there. As if only a soft wind were breezing by, not even a slight movement to the bar. I tried a second time. Counted off aaaaaaannnnnnd nuthin. It doesn't make sense, I just lifted this weight 6 times? "Maybe the

3rd time is a charm", I thought. Counted off and pushed and pushed and pushed and pushed and almost went to the bathroom in my Bugle-Boy workout pants (don't judge, there was an extreme amount of pushing involved). No matter how hard I tried, I could not budge that weight. The strange thing is, I had literally just lifted this same weight within the last 5 minutes. The amount of weight didn't change. The power of the person lifting the weight didn't change. The only thing that changed was the mindset. You see, even though I had just proved that I could lift the weight, my mind was so set on the boundary of the past that it immediately reverted back to that limit. Had I not known the amount of weight and we tried one more set, there is a good chance that I would have lifted that weight again. The mindset causes every other physical capability to cling to the CAN'T in your life. To this day, I still have never lifted as much weight as I did on that sacred day. I caught a glimpse of what is possible, and in my case, I don't necessarily need to have that super strength ability. Therefore, I stopped going for the goal of lifting incredible amounts of weight. I did, however, learn such a valuable lesson that day, we can do far more than we think we can. Who knows what limitations we are keeping ourselves bound to all because of CAN'T mentalities. Now please hear me, I am not saying to go to the gym this evening, stack a ton of weights on start shouting "I can do all things through Christ who strengthens me!", and start pressing. Chances are, you will end up in the hospital with a hernia. What I am saying is this. Overcoming the CAN'T mentality will take repetitive practice on a daily basis. We will find ourselves catching glimpses of the power we can walk in along the way. As we see these things, it doesn't mean we are completely out of the woods in that area but embrace it as God giving you a preview on just how much potential you have. Slow growth is healthy growth. It is never good to stretch so much all at once that it rips the muscle from the bone. Slight tears along the way mixed with correct healing after the workouts will produce gradual growth. This is the goal in breaking the CAN'T mentality.

Simple application:

1. Identify.
   What areas of your life are you immediately saying "I can't"? One of these areas could be the very thing God plans to use to bring glory to Him through you here on earth. Remember my story about the 5th grade teacher telling me I would never be able to speak to make a living. God had different plans, but it took me going out on a limb and exercising my weakness until it became a strength.
2. Stretch.
   You will never turn a CAN'T mentality into a CAN mentality without saying yes and trying. This is the equivalent of sitting down on the bench press and lifting. Important to get others around you that can coach you as you go, because if you are doing it right, everything in you will become sore shortly after you start. This will cause you to think that you are out of your

field and make you want to stop. After all, if this is what you are supposed to be doing, wouldn't it just flow with minimal pain involved? No. Anyone who works out correctly will be met with growing pains. This is from the stretch and tearing of the muscle. Don't stay away from the "I can" response just because you know there will be stretching involved. That is called laziness. Nothing worth having comes without work.

CHAPTER 4 – Fear of REJECTION

The fear of rejection is a strange thing. Most all of us say we don't care what other people think, yet, if that were true, we wouldn't demand to look at their phones to ensure that the picture they are about to post of us is "okay". The truth is, we all care about what others think. This is not unhealthy at its core, but it easily becomes something that can control our decisions and be the vital factors upon which we make choices. I recall one of the most, potentially embarrassing moments I had concerning the fear of being rejected. I warn you ahead of time, this story includes low-brow humor and content so fancy readers, please skip on to chapter 4. For those of you still left, let's dig in.

It was 11th grade, I was a transfer student at a new school. With no friends at the school, the desire to be there was very minimal. To add to my lack of friend issues at the time, I was also under, what I felt to be a heavy level of scrutiny. You see, as I mentioned in my prior book, Scars, my 11th grade year found me moving from an inner-city school of about 3000 students to a much smaller school out in the country with almost 300 students. My being half Mexican/half White boy at this new school meant I was 100 percent Mexican. And that was not too celebrated in this community during this time. I am sure it is a vision of multi-culturalism by now, I'm just saying THEN, not so much. The year was 1989 and MC Hammer pants where "in". At least at the former inner-city school. So when I showed up on campus of the new school, complete with stripes shaved into the sides of my hair and eyebrows, MC Hammer pants on, they didn't know what to think of the new guy. These are just some of the possible reasons the local students kept initial distance from me. And I get it. You want to be very careful about inviting someone new into your group too soon. There is a difference in being friendly and welcoming verses putting your entire hard earned reputation on the line. I mean, you gotta have a season of evaluation. Even jobs have a 30, 60 and 90 day review to make sure it's a fit. Well, I was on that evaluation period for sure and this was only the 2nd week. As I sat there quietly in my tiny plastic desk chair (the kind that form unseeable cracks that only open up as the weight of your body presses down on them, then, as you shift, you receive a pinch unlike anything you have ever experienced in life. Not cool plastic desk chair. Not cool at all.), I was trying desperately not to sneeze. You know the feeling, that conjuring of weird sinus pressure forming from the back of your upper neck area and slowly moving into the upper rear of your inner skull. Several times it had happened, yet no sneeze. I thought to myself, I need to get this thing out. So, reaching into my memory bank of different advice I have been given in life throughout my life, I searched for the sneeze category. As I wondered the memory halls I saw "Don't run with scissors" leaning against the locker talking to "Just breathe". Across the way, next to the doorway stood "lift with your legs" checking his phone and there outside in the cold was "Don't marry outside of your race". I couldn't even believe he was still alive, but apparently so. Then, like a beacon of hope, glimmering in the sun was the advice I was searching for, "Look at the light". Ah ha! The missing ingredient for my get this sneeze out recipe. Therefore, I took heed and wouldn't you know it, in only seconds, I felt the sneeze conjure from the back of my head toward the front. In the mean time, I was doing that strange thing we do with our face when we are about to sneeze. I don't care who you are or where you are from, this is an international, global expression we all make. I call it the "International I'm about to sneeze face". It is as if we just caught wind of the most horrific smell in the world while at the same time trying to bite an invisible apple hovering 3 inches in front of our face. After a few times of that unfortunate move, my body added the, what I like to call, "The international I'm about to sneeze noise". Now this is a bit harder to describe in book form, so you may need to pick up the audio version to get complete clarity. It is like as if an opera singer has taken control of only one section of your mouth and they are attempting to convince the rest of your head that you can sing a sudden majestic mid-tone vibrato for only 2 seconds. This renders us looking and sounding very cartoon character-ish. I sat there doing my best to look at the light while attempting to press through the face and noise distortion so that I could sneeze. Then, finally, after several seconds of trying, here came the good stuff. A sneeze of such magnitude that everything within me tensed up. Imagine having the actual ability to suck in enough air to put out a forest fire upon release, THAT is the kind of force this seemed to be. The one problem was this, there was so much wind that wanted to come out, it seemed to have become impatient. Half of the wind decided, "we can't wait to get out....We've gotta find another way out!". Yes, this means what you are thinking it means. I not only was sneezing but at the same time, my body was pushing out "wind" from anywhere it could. I didn't know if the release was loud because all I could hear was "AACHOOO". But what I do know about the moment is, my MC Hammer pants IMMEDIATELY inflated full of air. It was like watching someone hook a balloon up to a helium tank. There I sat, insecurity seeping toxic fumes from within the interior of the pants, out into the exterior. At that moment, I was so scared to be exposed as the person I really was, a gas monger. My fear was driven by the notion that, had anyone heard this accidental incident, I would be rejected. Fear of rejection is real! I know I know, this sounds a little low brow and extreme to use in a self-help, faith-based, leadership book, but don't blame me, I mean the title I went with is "New You verses the Screw You". The fact that I chose that title says something about me, the fact that you bought it says a little more about you. We may be a perfect literary match. How in the world could I have ever gone on another day had these people concluded that I was a person who had the audacity to pass gas and sneeze at the same time. I mean, surely I was the first person in history who EVER did this….right? No. Truth be told, the only reason you are enjoying this story so much is because you too have had this same exact, unexpected experience. And guess what, you lived. That is my point, we made it through in the past, we will make it through in the present and future.

The reason I use such simplicity to state this case has to do with the way we process mindset changes. We very rarely retain large factual foreign information and when we do, it is even more rare that we use that information to bring about habitual change. It is usually the small steps that slowly change the trajectory of our journey. And though this simple adjustment on small levels may not look like very much in the moment, over time, the place we end up is so far removed from the faulty course we were on in the past. Picture it like an airplane taking off. One spot is the starting point and the other is the final-destination (a term I am still very uncomfortable using in terms of air travel) point. If the pilot is one degree off in direction, at first, it will not be very noticeable. We will look out the window and see the same type of terrain all around us. If there is a flight tracker GPS in the plane, it will even show us in the same city. So what's the big deal with not fixing the small adjustment? Glad you asked, the further you go, the greater off course you will be. Eventually, you will be so far away from where you intended to arrive, you will have to land in another place all together. Many of us have found ourselves starting journeys with good intent. We felt ready for the journey and paid the price to fuel up. Problem is, the small adjustments needed on the front end weren't treated as important (mainly because they didn't seem large enough to matter). Then, there we were, time and time again, wondering why we seem to be so far away from our dreams and purpose. It is the small things! So how in the world does me passing gas and sneezing have anything to do with any of this? Because, you understand that in my life time, there would be things that came along that proved to be so much greater in size than the fear of being rejected by a bunch of people I didn't know for doing something I didn't even mean to do! But had I stayed at a mental place in my life to constantly be consumed with what others thought about silly things, I would never ever take public stands when they need to be taken. I can tell you, as a person of faith who works among the world of stand-up comedy, sometimes my beliefs are not exactly being celebrated by others from the stage. I am fortunate enough to be included in a very "secular" field as a communicator. If I were still at the place in my life where random gas accidents rendered me paralyzed with fear of rejection, I would never be able to speak with confidence and gain respect of others. Fear of rejection starts with Identifying the small, dealing with it over and over until it is not on your registry of fears any longer, then doing the same on the next level. There will always be new things and mentalities to conquer, but that is part of the fun. Because each time we do, it sets us on a straighter pathway to our destiny.

A few years ago, I was suspended from one of the 3 major social media sights for 48 hours. Perhaps this is the "persecution" that Jesus described that we would face for being his followers. I must admit, it is a little better than having my head chopped off like John the Baptist, or crucified upside-down like Peter. When I get to heaven, I am sure at some point there will be a Martyr gathering...I am not sure I will be let in the door as of yet. But nevertheless, I will share this story with you as it relates to today's culture. One morning, I woke up to about 2500 really mean messages. I swallowed my sip of coffee, cleared my throat, rubbed my eyes of the morning residue, and thought, "hmm, that's a little more than usual". Upon further investigation, I traced the thread back to a pretty famous person who wrote the original message "It's a shame that some of the most brilliant comedy writers in Hollywood today are still nieve enough to believe in the concept of God". Then they attached only one name to the post, my name. I guess along with that post, came a large amount of people ready to crucify the person that it was directed toward, once again, me. I had the audacity to respond by saying, "Dear _____ fans, (I leave out the name because I believe in the concept of covering people when they do something foolish that they may look back on and regret. People are much like Pigeons, bless them when they leave because they will most likely be returning. When they do, make it as easy as possible for them to come back without shame and embarrassment. We all act stupid from time to time so its best to extend grace.) I understand why you may be attacking me. You are _____ fans and believe in him and want to speak up on his behalf. Please realize that this is exactly what I am doing for my God." Pretty simple and kind right? I guess not. It would seem as if I took a stick from the yard and just started poking at a bee infested hive up in a reachable branch of a tree. Swarms of messages followed directed at me. Some of the most horrific cut downs I've ever faced. Some, I will admit were pretty funny so I wrote those ones down for my own personal files while others really swung at me hard. Note, NONE of these people knew me, yet they were saying mean things about my family, my faith, my hairline, there was no boundary. After all the dust settled on that day, I had about 11 thousand messages directed toward me. The sight sent me notification that I was being suspended for 48 hours because there was too much negative traffic coming FROM my page!? I was thinking, "_____ was bullying me!". But it didn't really matter. You see, in the past, the old, timid, frail, thin skinned Elijah Tindall would've been greatly affected by this. But not now. I have, over time, been conditioned to handle rejection. My fear of what people think has greatly minimized. The classroom gas passing moments only proved to serve as skin thickening experiences to prepare me for the days I would face "persecution". The silliness of this situation is stated early, when I joked about the Disciples gathering around sharing their persecution stories while I bring up the fact that I was suspended from social media for 2 days. Our definition of persecution, here in the United States, is sure different than what they faced in history. We see things as so bad in this culture while we literally have the right to worship our God every weekend in open door forums. This isn't even close to persecution friends. I fear, however, that if we actually were faced with true persecution, we would be far from the place we need to be in terms of readiness. Our self-consumed culture would most likely be too busy taking selfies to know what to do or how to handle it. We are busy posting pictures of our worship to show how cool we look in smoke and high dollar lighting while other cultures are facing dismemberment and death to even speak the name that we try to avoid using too much of on stage in hopes that we don't run off a first-time guest. Now I know this doesn't apply to you, but most likely to too many of the people around you. I do not intend any disrespect toward anyone's method of reaching a lost culture in saying all this either. I, myself am very careful when it comes to how I share my faith as I am called to drive in a very unique lane on this journey. It seems as if I have been given favor with both God and with man in many ways. I do not want to run off the people that God is using me to bring to him by foolish statements or stances that really are more current pop or political culture than they are kingdom. This is why we must look at our own calls and assignments and determine the best way to condition ourselves in the areas in which we could face rejection. For me, working with both church and unchurched, I face potential rejection in any conversation I have of topics spanning from sexual identity, tattoos on a Christian, speaking in tongues, eating meat to foolish jesting. Believe it or not, each of these topics mentioned have shown up on my message board as heated discussion people wanted to argue with me over. And I am not just talking about the unchurched crowd. What you have to do is, as the scripture states, "Study to show thyself approved". This means, your confidence comes from your assurance in studying out and gaining an understanding of what God's word says about the topics that relate to your call. Some things will not be a huge part of the assignment you are called to. So, in those cases, when people reject you, it isn't that devastating of a feeling. For example, I am just not a person with a passion to teach on end times. Many are, and you can tell by their verbiage within moments. From the abundance of the heart, the mouth speaks, and their mouth speaks of tribulation periods, armagedon, raptures and horses with heavenly riders ascending from the sky. My mouth on the other hand, not so much. End times is not a passion of mine. Not because it holds little value, it is just as important as any other subject in the bible, but rather because it is not pertinent to the assignment I am designed to accomplish here on earth. You will find me being more interested in "Be ye kind one to another" than the beast with 7 horns or the Desolation of Isolation. Why? Because my assignment is to help bridge the gap between a non-believing culture and a loving God. Things like, "By this, all will know that you are my disciples, by the love you show, one to another." Why is that important to me, because when we show love toward each-other, it lifts up the name of Jesus and he said, "If my name be lifted up, I will draw all men unto me". My goal is to get them drawn to him. That being said, there are those that want to have scripture interpreted to them before they would ever consider following my God. For those people, my kind of evangelism will most likely not work. This is why its important that each believer play their part in who they are called to be. Each joint, fitly put together, as it is written. Once we identify the nature of the call we have, it is easier to target the kinds of areas to strengthen and condition ourselves in to guard against the fear of rejection. If someone rejects me for my views on end times, who cares, it doesn't bother me that much. Because truth be told, don't tell anybody this, but I could very well be wrong. Heck, I don't know it all and that stuff seems very confusing to me. Now, if I am rejected over defending a person who is lost while I am trying to navigate them into the kingdom, this I will get very upset and sideways about. That is my passion. Therefore, that is where the enemy will attack me the hardest. He knows that if he can cause me to get all ruffled up and bothered in the area of my call, I will not walk in it correctly. You can't walk in your call and in anger, frustration and un-peace at the same time. Not having authority over the fear of rejection will cause you to always overthink what others MAY be thinking about you. And most of the time, they aren't thinking about you at all.

Sign of insecurity:
A good way to identify whether or not you are insecure in the area of rejection is to think back to when you may have posted a status or commented on someone elses post online. If someone commented something that conflicted with your statement on that post,

1. How did you feel?
   Feelings are emotional indicators of what is on the inside. Was it a heated frustration or a peaceful smirk? Pay very close attention to your feelings, for they speak louder to us than we care to admit. We often don't know we are insecure toward rejection because we constantly surround ourselves with those who think like us. We post or say things in circles that agree with our mentality, so when these moments arise, they are great learning opportunities. There is always room to grow, our measure if discomfort is the scale upon which we measure just how much. The less comfortable we feel when being rejected or confronted, the more growth we need. This does not mean we are wrong, it only means we

aren't as internally healthy and strong as we considered ourselves to be.

2. How did you respond?

Did you attempt to defend? If so, how did you go about it? Remember the story of Jesus. Toward the end of his journey here on earth, He told the disciples that he would be going away soon. They (specifically Peter) took issue with when he talked like this. His intention was always to defend Jesus, yet his godly nature wasn't fully developed just quite yet. He didn't know that, he thought he was all good (much like us). One night, the Roman soldiers were told where Jesus was hanging out, they where given the assignment to go get him. Upon arrival, Peter gets all social justice warrior and grabs one of the guard's swords and literally takes a swing. He hits a guy named Malcus. Now, in all of the portrayals of this scene, we always see these soldiers as evil guards on assignment to do the devils work. Let me suggest to you that they, much like any other military young men, were simply there serving in their armed forces. We, here in the U.S. rarely think of our military personnel as "bad guys". I am sure that the parents of these soldiers felt the same. These are just their kids, of age, serving their land and citizens. And on this night, a soldier named Malcus was given the assignment to join a few others and go escort a man named Jesus to courthouse. He didn't necessarily have evil contempt in his heart. Possibly even a wife and kid back at the house, who knows. Then, after the long haul to the area Jesus was in, he is met with a crazy eyed man swinging a sword and then wouldn't you know it, his ear gets cut off. Oye Vay, The bible says that Jesus, immediately rebukes Peter. Now wait a minute. How can it be that Jesus' rebuke is toward the guy who believes in him and is defending righteousness? That is a great question that we really need to seek the answer to in this day and time. Jesus' frustration was not with the one siding against him, but rather with the one who was already his follower. Here is a consideration, since Jesus said he came to seek and save that which was lost, perhaps, when being face to face with the "lost", he prefers that those who are his followers not attack them. The proof of this is in his next action. Jesus bends down and picks up the severed ear, places on the side of Macus' head, and heals the wound. What a great analogy of the churches current state in this world right now. At the first sign of rejection, we seem to be lashing out with our verbal swords toward those who are lost. We do this thinking that we are justified because we are protecting our beliefs, yet we do it in such a way that it is severing the potential for them to ever hear any sort of communication from the very God that we say we wish they would follow. The truth is, this has very little to do with us defending Jesus. It is a fear based knee-jerk response to them attacking us. This means we are walking in our identity and not in his. Jesus knew the soldiers were coming and he even warned them that it would happen, yet instead of being at the same level of peace he was with allowing others to reject him at the moment, Peter made it about flexing his physical ability to fight. In this case, Jesus was there to heal and restore communication between he and Malcus. I wonder how many ears we have cut off by our sword swinging responses due to our inability to handle the notion of personal rejection. My prayer is that somewhere down the road, Jesus is there, holding the bloody ear that we (me, not you, I know you are not guilty of this…just me), cut off. The interesting thing about this story is how only hours later, this same, sword swinging, good ole' American style Peter, stood in a public setting denying he even knew Jesus. Talk about wishy-washy. I would blame him had I not seen this very thing far too many times. We take these great declarations for our beliefs, spiritual highs followed by physical lows. We assume others are the wrong ones for rejecting us so we lash out, yet God is interested in growing us internally so we stop going on the attack toward the ones he wants to reach. I am not saying that there is not a time for standing up and defending, but I am saying we need to be wise in the way this is done. Any time we operate out of insecurity, we end up cutting off ears. If our goal is to truly do the work of the kingdom here on earth, we must allow the kingdom to grow in us and flow through us. Great news, even after Peter did all his shenanagans, Jesus appeared to him and called him to be the founding rock upon which we would build his church. Think about that, the foundation of the church is saturated with forgiveness and restoration. Just the kind of thing we need to hear after reading this chapter and identifying with cutting off all these folks ears.

Simple Application:
1. Identify:
   What are the areas within your calling that you seem to be overly defensive about? You cant strengthen that area without being honest about having insecurities in it.

2. Start small:
   Deal with things on a small level to condition for the bigger yet to come. Doesn't sound like rocket science but I can guarantee you, in the moments of discomfort, this point becomes harder but the internal peace you will walk in will be the evidence that your strength is growing. There will be a time when the things that bother you now will be so far removed from your radar, and in that day, you will, like Jesus, be the one restoring communication between God and those that persecute and criticize Him. Internal strength is what He is interested in and a fear of rejection will hold you back from living out the new you.

Chapter 5 – ATTITUDE

The year was 1987, I received my workers permit the day I turned 14 and marched my long haired self-up to the doors of Burger King to fill out an application. I had a string to pull that would help me get the much-wanted entry level position from the inside. You see, my older sister already worked there. She talked to the manager, I got the permit and bada-bing bada-bang, I was the new hire on my way up the corporate ladder. One stipulation, I had to get my hair cut. Once again, this was the mid/later 80's and glam was everything to me. The only thing bigger to me than my long-term dream of making it as either a Rock drummer or Rapper (ET Fresh), was my immediate dream of buying a car. You may be thinking, you were only 14, you couldn't even drive yet. This is true, but I had the foresight to know that if I wanted to drive a car when I turned 16, I needed to get a job, so I could save up to buy one, thus, the workers permit. I went to the local beauty school - of which I am always a big fan of because you never really know what haircut you may walk out with – , I told them, I need my hair cut for a job in the food industry. The "stylist" looked at my glorious 16-inch mane spiked 6 inches tall on the top and reaching well below the middle of my back, and said, "I know the perfect cut!". 15 minutes later, I walked out with a complete level 2 clipper cut. My ears protruded at least 3 inches from both sides of my head...I hadn't seen those things in years. I was very saddened, but it was for the sake of the greater cause. I put on my rust brown uniform, nervously opened the right front door of the establishment and that is when I first met Fred.

Fred was a 6 foot 4-inch-tall, 16-year-old young man. The smile on his face was genuine and when he said he would be training me, I felt at ease. Something about the way he talked just felt soothing. It was as if Fred was THE Burger King. But he wasn't. As time went by, I begin to learn the stories of my fellow workers. Something about working jobs together forms a unique bond in between people. Even if you work with someone you don't care for, there is a shared comradery, just by being in the war of the workplace together. I learned that Fred's background was filled with almost every kind of struggle one could face. He lived in an area we called, Sin City. It was one of the roughest neighborhoods in the Little Rock area. I also learned two more very important points for this story. 1, The cool gangsta limp that Fred walked with was not intentional at all. Fred, in his childhood, had an accident that cost him the lower part of his right leg. From the knee down, Fred had a prosthetic leg. And 2, Fred had an identical twin brother named Darryl. While Fred walked with a gangsta-limp out of injury, Darryl did not. Darryl's walk looked gangsta because he WAS gangsta. He was wrapped up in all kinds of crime on a regular basis. Problem was, because these two were identical, it was almost impossible to tell them apart until you talked to them. Fred had such a positive demeanor and attitude at all times while Darryl seemed to take on the identity of a victim in life. It was interesting because, though both grew up in the same exact environment and difficult set of circumstances, they both chose different roads when it came to their attitude about life. As I would think about all the things that they were faced with, my mind and heart would gravitate toward Darryl. It was easy to understand, based on the absence of parents, physical abuse from adults in some of the most humiliating ways a person could experience and living conditions, why one would take on a bad attitude toward life. I would not blame Darryl for some of choices he made, even if they were wrong, I tended to have a sort of compassion toward him. That is, until you were in the presence of Fred. For whatever reason, Fred chose to take on a positive attitude about life. Never once did I hear him complain, not once. It made me feel a sense of conviction just being around him. I would complain about part of my check needing to go to help pay a bill, while he was using his entire check to feed his younger siblings and cousins. Yet, not a peep of negativity. Being around him just made you a better person by the end of the shift. He was always positive. Not only was he an overcomer in his attitude toward life, but he also did whatever he could to help others. I failed to mention that Fred was also a black-belt in Taekwondo. He got permission to use the dojo once a week to teach neighborhood kids the martial arts for free. In an inner-city area like this one, this was a much-needed form of discipline as well as defense. So, there he was, every Saturday morning, teaching 5-12-year old's Taekwondo, while Darryl was most likely trying to post bail downtown. Both looked alike, walked alike, shared the same exact history, yet one chose a positive attitude while the other a negative one. I am crying laughing as I sit here and think on the only time I ever saw Fred not smile. We were both working on a Friday night. I was on register taking customer's orders (which is a very important position for me to be in because it was one of the only 2 places that provided a microphone. As you may remember, my dream was to be a rapper…ET Fresh). My rap crew partner, Rawdacious Roy was working drive through (once again, perfect. He was mainly in charge of providing the beatboxing in the crew). The only time we were allowed to open the mic up was when someone would order a chicken sandwich. At which point we would both give each other the look, grip mics and rip mics. The guys in the kitchen would dance in celebration to our funky fresh style of ordering. Between me and Roy was Fred. He was in the "expedite" position. This mainly consisted of taking the food off the slide down burger holder and placing the food, fries and drinks onto the tray, then giving the tray to the customers. He was perfect in this role because of how friendly he was. If anything communicated giving the customer food "their way", it was Fred handing you the tray with a genuine smile on his face. There we were, in the middle of a dinner rush when we heard/felt a slam. We all looked at each other because, at this point, none of us knew where the sound was coming from. It happened again, then once more. The fluid in the cups seemed to spill over the top as if an earthquake was happening in a rhythmic pattern, that's when we saw him. If Fred was 6'4, this man must've stood a minimum of 6 foot 9. His shirt seemed to fade into patches of skin in some areas. As if they were one, it was like an optical illusion only, not. I am confident of what I saw, I may not have clarity on what exactly it was, but I am confident of the experience. I can't imagine what size of overalls these were that fit his giant body, but they looked like they had been worn for a minimum of 8 years. He smelled as if he consumed and entire liquor store on the way to the Burger King. Not a bottle, not an aisle, but the entire store....and a large store at that. Breaking through the middle of the rush hour line, he began to mutter, "I said no lettuce". No one dared to stop him, "I SAID NO LETTUCE". His volume increased to a threatening sounding level. As he reached the counter, directly in front of Fred, his shadow cast upon us and a blistering cold artic wind accompanied, at least that's how it felt in the moment. He looked at Fred standing there with a smile on his face and shouted, once more, "I SAID NO LETTUCE"! Fred, looking at the Whopper in the palm of his giant hand and replied, "I'm so sorry sir, let me have the cooks make you a fresh burger immediately.". As Fred started to turn toward the kitchen, the tree of a man, reached out and grabbed Fred by the collar with both hands. Fred attempted to continue to smile, but when the rag-doll style of shaking started, it became impossible. I remind you, Fred is a tall young man. Yet this Neanderthal had the ability to lift him off the ground, into the air and shake him all while shouting, "I SAID NO LETTUCE", with ease. This was bad. I concluded 2 things. 1, Fred is most likely going to lose at least one more leg today, and 2, this gentleman did NOT like lettuce. As he continued to shake Fred, it was impossible to ignore the Jerry Curl juice Fred used on his hair flying all over the perimeter. There were 2 main hair products back in the 80's. One was Aqua-Net and the other was Jerry Curl juice. I think at one point I even saw a cook catch some mid-air with a hamburger bun. "Secret sauce", I thought to myself. Finally, he let Fred go. As Fred began to make his way back onto the ground, a strange thing happened, Fred landed in the Kung-Fu position. Oh no, I whispered. Me and Rawdacious Roy met eyes. The only thing we could offer in a such a time as this was a funky fresh rhyme, but it just didn't seem right. We were all standing there paralyzed in fear. All of us except for Fred. There he stood, across the counter with a serious look on his face. His hair a bit dryer than 5 minutes earlier and his stance in the classic L martial arts form. We all could sense what he was about to do. Before we could stop him, his right leg lifted off the ground, his body twisted, and a solid roundhouse kick was being executed across the Burger King counter. This was quite the Friday night so far. The moment Fred fully extended the move – pay attention because this is where it gets good – FRED'S LEG FLEW OFF. Yep, you read that correctly, the lower half of Fred's leg somehow came out of its prosthetic socket and flew directly into the shake master's upper left shoulder. It wasn't forceful enough to do any damage, but I can only imagine that whatever the giant drank before he got there that night, it wasn't even close to enough to keep him from immediately sobering up. I've heard of 12 steps, but this was a literal foot. No one knew what to look at. Do we look at the giant, standing there dumbfounded? Do we look at Fred, with pantleg dangling as he balanced on one leg while maintaining eye contact with the mutant or do we look at the spinning wooden leg in the middle of the line, surrounded by crying children and families that appeared to have just been in a natural disaster. I don't remember exactly how that incident ended, all I know is, this was a side of Fred I had never seen before. But at least this attitude shift was due to protecting himself. The next day, even later that night, Fred had reset himself back to Homeplate, a kind, peaceful attitude. As years went by, I saw Fred at a shopping mall during Christmas season. I recognized him immediately. He stood there in the Santa line being climbed like a tree by his 2 toddler children. I was visiting family back in Arkansas, by this time, I had moved to Oklahoma City to pursue a Youth Pastor position. I think it was a bit harder for him to recognize me as my hair had grown from the short level 2 buzz to what was now over 5 years' worth of dreadlocks. Once he did make the connection he jumped fully into the conversation. We covered years of progress and updates while reminiscing over Burger King memories. In a discrete way, he mentioned that his brother, Darryl had passed. I tried to be as compassionate as possible while maintaining discretion in front of his family. It seems like his involvement in gang life resulted in him serving time in prison and tragically, the day he was released, he was also brutally murdered. That is a lot of information to take in while talking to an old friend in a Santa Clause line. Fred showed respect and honor with his words, but I could tell, this ending was no surprised. It was the same track his had taken and lord knows this story is no stranger to young men in poverty-stricken communities. Fred, however had a very different end result. The love and life on his face shone brighter than ever. As he looked at his kids, I couldn't help but to look at him. How in the world could someone who has been through so much have such a positive attitude? Commitment, that is the answer. There is no way that Fred could have chosen to take on a positive attitude through all these obstacles had it not been that he was highly committed to force himself down that road. It is much easier to take the negative attitude exit in life. The more unfair situations we are faced with, the more opportunities there are to fall into a victim mentality. After all, most all of us can justify this direction. I mean, we've all been done wrong in some way over time. The thing is, God has given us free-will to choose either one. It is up to us. If we want to wallow around in the mud that is our situation and past, we have permission. God will not stop us. He loves us equally as much either way. So why wouldn't we? It is, after all, the easier thing to do. The answer is, end result. Though God is permissive of our justified rotten attitudes, others are not. And it is others that must live with us. Over time, people become very unsettled around negative people. The result of a negative attitude is isolation. We find ourselves gradually become lonelier and lonelier. Friend groups turn into friends turn into friend turn into binging Netflix alone every weekend or late nights mid-week. Of all the readers of this book, I realize that 99.9 percent will not have a relatable life experience to that of Darryl and Fred. Their circumstances were extreme, but their attitude choice options were the same as anyone else's. Good attitude verses bad attitude. Scripture reminds us that God has placed before you the option to choose life or to choose death, it then suggests that we choose life. Why? Because that is what Jesus claims to have come to give us. "The thieve comes to steal, kill and destroy. But I have come to give you life and life more abundant." John 10:10. A bad attitude will never be the pathway to an abundant life. The notion may seem to indicate that, if one chooses a good attitude, external problems will cease to exist. As we saw with Fred, that isn't necessarily the case. It is very possible that even with a good attitude, we find ourselves subject to things out of our control. What we do gain, however, is an internal peace, as that is what produces the abundance of life. I have seen billionaires surrounded by material treasure yet still not happy, while on the other hand, someone who struggles greatly to make ends meet, smiling with a peace that no amount of money can purchase. I, personally, would prefer to be a billionaire with an internal peace, but if I must choose only one of those things, I would rather start with the peace that comes along with an attitude adjustment. There are sure tell signs as to whether you are experiencing the symptoms of a bad attitude.

Symptoms of Bad Attitudes

1. Blame:
    A person with a bad attitude always points at other people or things as a reason for their situation. Their points are often very valid, yet the longer they see others as the issue, they keep themselves bound to the position of a victim. You can't do anything about others, but you can do something about your attitude toward them.

2. Isolation:
    A person with a bad attitude will almost always be on the decreasing side of friendships. No one enjoys being around complainers. Good friends and long-time relationships will begin to gradually fade. If you see this happening, it is most likely not them… it may be you.

3. Losing out on opportunities:
    A person with a bad attitude will not be offered promotion as much as someone who is positive. Higher positions require greater leadership skills. A great leader will be someone who attracts people rather than repels them. When choosing someone for a leadership role, we look at what their personality is like, because we know that is what will be reproduced into the employees or volunteers under them. Negative attitudes almost immediately disqualify a person from being

considered for promotion. If you feel like you have been overlooked for a promotion or opportunity, you may want to consider if your attitude is the kind that would be celebrated if the whole company acted in the same way. I'm sure it is, but, ya know, just sayin.

Once again, choosing to have a good attitude may not stop bad things from happening in your life. It will however determine the quality of life you have while walking through hard seasons. I have had several things come my way that were very hard to live through, some I met with a positive, optimistic response, while others, not so much. On every occasion that I choose the negative route, I ended up having to stop somewhere along the way and say, "I can't live like this", and decided to make the internal adjustment to choosing good. It wasn't easy, but it was necessary if I was going to ever have peace. Believe me, going through divorce, losing a home, waking up in seizures due to diabetic reactions, having a quadruple bypass and so much more that I haven't even scratched the surface on, is not easy and in many ways gives me an excuse to take on a negative attitude, but it doesn't help me. That is what I want you to understand. In all this, the simple message is, it doesn't help you. The thing that will screw you up in life, causing you to be the Screw You, is a bad attitude. Yes, we can dig in deeper to the theology which declares what you believe, you say, and what you say, you will eventually have (This means that if you believe things to always be negative, you will start speaking negative and in return, you will end up producing negative results.). But, all you need to really embrace is that the feeling of a bad attitude alone will have you walking through hell on earth before each day even starts. It is not worth it. As I sit here writing this very line, I am faced with an opportunity to take on a bad attitude mentality. A couple of weeks ago, I had a trip in which my suitcase was lost. Inside that suitcase sat my computer. And inside that computer sat the completed version of this very book. The only version. While, yes, I was saving each chapter as I wrote, I was NOT, however, doing what I did on the first book, which is to email myself and the fellow editors a copy. I now find myself "in the press", as they say. My release date is less than 3 weeks from now and I have plenty of other projects on my plate, each with their own deadline. I can either wave my fist in the air and post negative comments toward the company that lost my suitcase, or I can take a moment, breathe, press reset and acknowledge that no matter how much I spew negativity toward others, it does not resolve my problem. I must put my nose to the grindstone and get to work. I needed a new computer to do so. Well, with 4 kids, 2 adults and 3 pets in the house, the budget didn't exactly have the cushion we needed to absorb this purchase. "How do I make it happen", I thought to myself. I started reflecting on the principles I teach in this book. 1, CAN. I had to force myself to take on a CAN mentality. This CAN happen.

I have the contents in my spirit and computers do exist, all I need is access to one. 2, Fear of Rejection. I had to convince myself that even if the book is released a week or 2 later then announced, my followers and friends would be understanding. They would not reject me over this, and if they did, I can easily return their initial money they may have sent for a Pre-Sale discount. This is a doable situation. And 3 (I applied points 4 and 5 also but have yet to introduce those to you so I want to do a spoiler here. You can turn the pages and look for yourself if you are an impatient person), Attitude. I purposely chose to take on a good attitude. I can't change what has happened, but I can change my attitude toward it. Once I make that adjustment, it allows me to see the options for moving forward. The fact that you are reading this book proves that it worked. Within 24 hours, My sister (the murderous one from chapter 3 of my last book, SCARS) contacted me and told me that she and her husband, Justin, (my brother-in-law) needed a logo made for their new venture. I used to be a free-lace graphics artist, it's what kept my family afloat when I left a full-time staff position at a church in Oklahoma and merged into the world of stand-up comedy. We discussed pricing but I told her that it may be a while due to my computer being lost and possibly gone forever. They quickly through Justin's year-old laptop into the mix of negotiations. This was perfect! While I was believing for the best-case scenario of my suitcase being found and returned with my laptop and all my chapters inside, I had to prepare for the possibility of it being gone. This gave me the ability to start over. Within a day, I loaded Word (I'm a PC man. Sorry MAC folks, I know I said I was a designer and that seems to conflict but PC's just make more sense to me. And yes, I am fully aware that I have now been disqualified by over half the readers, it's okay. You must be who you are in life, and I am a PC guy. I can handle the firestorm of criticism, what I cannot handle is no right click on the mouse.) and typed the words, CHAPTER 1. Choosing a good attitude gave me options to move forward. Sure, I had to put in work, but that is just life. I've found that the more work you invest into a project, the more you appreciate the end-result. Friend, I don't know what circumstances life has handed you. Chances are, you have great reason to justify any, and all negative statements and point blame. I do know, however, that bad attitude will be the leash upon which you bind yourself. It will hold you back just like it has every person who committed to it in the past. You and I are no exceptions. We too will be subject to the results of releasing a negative spirit into this atmosphere. So, just like God suggested to His people, I suggest to you, choose life.

Chapter 6 – ZEAL *(lack of)*

Warning, this chapter is exclusively for the "Believers", those of us who claim to be Christ Followers, AKA, Christians. While it will be good exposure to all others as to how a Christian should think, it does not apply for various reasons. Do not feel excluded by this, in fact, I encourage you to read through and investigate the content. It will be helpful while at the same time, non-applicable to your life.

Have you ever been handed a color sheet portraying Jesus swinging around a whip like Zorro while kicking at people and turning tables full of money over? No? Me neither. In all my life of growing up in church, never have I ever seen a kid running out of children's church with this paper. I've seen sheets with wet glue and sloppily placed glitter leaving a trail from the classroom to the sanctuary. I've seen shell covered pieces of construction paper mixed with pop-sickle sticks, but not once the fighting Jesus. Usually, our portrayal of Jesus is that of a kind faced, gentle person holding a lamb, surrounded by children, cooking enchiladas for the disciples, but never throwing kicks. Why? Because this was not his natural personality. He was the definition of "peace-maker." Yet, we do find one story that does see him in this, rap video type of persona. It was when He and the disciples walked into the temple one day. They looked around to see money-changers at tables doing business. Trading, selling, promoting the latest products at the merch table. Jesus did something at that moment that surprised everyone. He started weaving together straps of leather to make a whip. Now, even though he was a carpenter by trade, I can only imagine that Jesus, the creator of EVERYTHING, could make a solid whip. His weaving skills are probably on point. If I had corn-rolled hair, I would want Jesus to be the stylist. There he stood, weaving the leather strips together. I can only speculate his countenance while doing this, perhaps he made eye contact with a few people. I would hate to be one of those people. Literally looking into the face of an angry, frustrated God. "Oh, don't you worry, I can bring you back to life", he may mutter in my direction. No thanks. I am glad I was not present in that day and time. The story goes on to say that he turned the money tables over in frustration. Can you imagine? This kind, gentle, peace-mongerer of a man, suddenly flipping out, making whips, kicking tables over and chasing people around the foyer until they left or safely hid under the sink in the restroom. How different of a Jesus is this!? This didn't match the description we knew Jesus to be at all. Yet, something inside his spirit was set off by what he walked in and saw. John 2:17 states, His disciples remembered that is was written: "Zeal for your house will consume me."

Zeal is defined as: Great energy or enthusiasm in pursuit of a cause or an objective.

Consumed is defined as: Absorb all the attention and energy.

Let's read that scripture with those words defined inside the text: His disciples remembered that it was written, Great energy and enthusiasm in pursuit of your house will absorb all my energy. That begins to shine light on why Jesus' normal, everyday personality changed on this day. When He explained to the boys, "Seek first the kingdom of God, and all these other things will be added to you". He laid out a template for them (and us) to live our lives by. Our seeking God's house/kingdom should be a passion that burns within us. Zeal toward God's house is one of the biggest mindsets we must embrace as believers if we are to ever walk in the **New You** identity. Our center is meant to be God's kingdom and out of that filters the rest of everything our life touches. Many times, especially with us men, we use the excuse that it's just not our personality to be expressive in things like worship during church. While this may be true, the interesting thing in this story is how, when it came to what took place in His Father's house, Jesus chose to take on a different personality. Zeal for the kingdom consumed him. I have never been a giant sports fan. At best, I'm a poser. I root for teams based on where they are from and their logo. I know, I don't deserve a man card. I have seen guys who are into sports. Some of my best friends and even my son, is quite passionate about their teams. I will not criticize them for this. I think it is healthy to have things you enjoy rooting for. I will not go into a religious schpill here and start pointing out how if you can remember all the stats from the team's history, you could surely memorize a few scriptures. I won't do that because it doesn't cause you to adjust toward God. What it does is cause you to view the things of God as a competition with things that you naturally enjoy. As if God was needing us to stop enjoying life to make room for Him. Not at all. God has created us to be people of abundance. We are designed to be expansive beings that grow in capacity as we embrace new things and thoughts. Us liking and enjoying other things does not steal from God. It is a limited mentality that teaches otherwise. Resent will quickly set in under that teaching. Condemnation never works to change behavior, it only causes someone to avoid us, so they don't have to feel fake for being people who enjoy things outside of what is going on beyond the church doors. Once I understand this, I can stretch my thinking from me being locked to a certain, pre-defined type of person inside God's house. I think it is great that people enjoy things. I see a custom chopper and my eyes light up. I can tell you different facts about motors, frames, pipes and gas tanks when it comes to Harley-Davidsons. This does not mean I don't love God. The only thing it does is show that there is a potential to operate at a higher level concerning other areas of my life. Perhaps I can go to another level beyond my "normal" self when it comes to church and God's kingdom. Jesus' natural personality was not known to be that of a thunderous, expressive person. Yet, when he walked into the temple, all bets were off. When we walk into God's house, we should walk in with a Zeal that consumes us. Our quest for things being in the right order – Kingdom first -, should be an active pursuit of our heart. As a person who has worked on staff at churches and still works with churches across the United States and abroad, I can tell you, this, sadly is not the case in most places. It is not just the congregants. So many of the places I have been seem to have a lack of zeal for God's house. Sure, we say the right things, use the right language but, if we were honest with ourselves, the zeal we exude is mostly by faith or by routine and technique. We have perfected scripts that produce results but that doesn't mean the passion is there. I can be a tree that produces apples, or I can go to the grocery store and purchase apples. To the person I give the apples to, it may not make that much of a difference, but to me, if I am called to be planted and produce apples, it makes all the difference in the world. We are kingdom people, transformed from darkness and into light. The produce that should come as a result is a zeal for kingdom things. Yet, I am concerned that we are just going to other conferences, event and services, buying apples then handing them to our congregation. This doesn't just apply to clergy/pastoral roles. The ministry is something we are all called to. Whether we be an electrician, nail technician, tattoo artist, business person, investor or anything else under the sun, all believers have a ministry call and assignment to BE a witness (Acts 1:8). Part of being a witness is having a passion for that which we say we love. If I see people miserable when they discuss marriage, it does not draw me to believe that marriage is a positive thing. Same goes for our relationship with God. These 2 things are supposed to be the most intimate of all a person can have, yet these are the 2 areas that most people seem very unhappy about. Their spiritual relationship and their marriage. This is a ripple that carries far beyond the intimate and into every aspect of life. The center of a believer's life is meant to be their relationship with God. The next thing is their spouse then their work and friendships. If we have lost zeal for kingdom, it will show up in all other areas. First, the marriage will suffer. If I can't be passionate toward my God, who created me, I will not have the ability to love and have passion for my spouse. Next the rest of my relationships, jobs and life issues will deteriorate. I venture to say, if you are feeling mediocre in the state of your marriage, it may stem from a lack of zeal you have toward your relationship with God. If this is the case, you most likely will not be drawn to be actively present in your church. To be clear, I am not saying that you must be an active part of a local church to experience a closeness and zeal for God. If that were the case, many prisoners, traveling business people, musicians, service industry workers and even evangelists would be incapable of intimacy with God. I am saying, however, that God's kingdom is best represented on earth by the local church. I view the local church as a parallel to the college classroom. You do not have to come to class. A price has already been paid for your position as a student. The teacher/professor is teaching the information for the test coming up in the class. Whether you are there or not, the test is still coming and there is a place where the answers to pass to the test is being taught. When the day comes, and the test is handed out, you cannot blame the professor for you failing the test. The information has been given to those in attendance, we just may've not chosen to be present. God gives his pastors and leadership the content for the tests coming up in our lives. This is why it's important to find the right church for you. If you feel like you are constantly being tested and find yourself failing over and over, maybe it's because you aren't going to class...just saying. And, if possible, going a step beyond, plugging in and serving the community through the local church is a great way to stir the pot and get some zeal brewing in life. Once again, the church is NOT God, but it is a representation of who He is in this world to others. If you ask an un-churched person where God's kingdom is, they will most likely point you to the nearest or most familiar church. It's a good idea to serve the people of your community through the avenue of your church. Serving doesn't guarantee that you will have zeal, but I can guarantee you that zeal is impossible to have without serving. Serving is the nature of God, therefore, the closer you get to Him, the more you act like Him. Remember Jesus saying, "I only do what I see my father in heaven do". He was one with the Father, therefore, he operated with zeal when it came to His father's house. He spent his entire life building the kingdom so when he walked in and saw it being misused, his passion took over.

So, what if you, like most people, are in the position of not having a zeal for God's house. It is not because you hate or are against God, it just doesn't seem to be there. Much like Peter telling Jesus, "help our unbelief". If that describes you, let me share a way to kickstart the process in getting that passion going.

1. **Serve – SACRIFICE FOR ATTACHES VALUE TO**

   I know that I said serving is a bi-product of having a zealous spirit, but it is also a method of attaining the same spirit. There is a principle I have mentioned before called "Sacrifice FOR attaches value TO". In other words, I will value what I sacrifice for. As recently as today, I muttered the words, "These kids don't respect this truck". I said it as I dug trash out from under the seat. The kids were not present, or I would've had them come clean it out, nevertheless, I, grudgingly gathered and carried the trash from the truck to the trash can. What does this have to do with our point? glad you asked. Because Stephanie and I work hard to pay the monthly payments and insurance on the vehicle, We treat it differently than others. My kids have not had to conjure jobs to pay the hundreds of dollars it takes to have this truck, and because of that, they don't think twice about leaving a piece of trash in it. The quickest way to cause them to value keeping the vehicle clean is for me to have them come out and clean it. The harder they must work to clean it will play in favor of their future cleanliness when it comes to this truck. Their sacrifice to clean it up and out will attach a value to it. The greatest thing we can do when we lack zeal is to serve. Serving will require sacrifice and that sacrifice will add value. The less zeal you have right now, possibly the better on the other side of the sacrifice. It will take more but you will value in a much deeper way. What is the last thing you sacrificed for God's house? It could be in the area of finances (perhaps your schedule doesn't allow you to be present for services very often), time (maybe your only day off is on a Sunday. This makes it hard to commit to giving up rest for church. It is a sacrifice) or several other ways. I don't know your church, I don't know your schedule or situation, but what I do know is that if you want to be a person with zeal, you must first plant seeds. As you do, you will find that the investment is building up and while others sit complaining about things, you will take personal responsibility for answering and speaking up, because you value the house you have helped build. Your sacrifice builds up into a value that will not stay silent in the presence of God's house being used in the wrong way or shone in the wrong light. You may find yourself turning over money tables where you used to not care one bit. Investment makes all the difference. Sacrifice **for** attaches value **to**.

2. Taking on a leadership role
    The difference between this and servanthood, is the taking on of responsibility to lead others in servanthood. We never leave the position of servant. It was Jesus' role and as His followers, it is to ours. Anyone who assumes leadership is beyond servanthood is a positional leader and will not be effective in the kingdom.

    I go to a Zumba class. Yes, you read that correctly, I. Go. To. Zumba. If you are unaware of what Zumba is, well, take a moment to look it up. When you get back you will be chuckling at the thought of me dancing around in Latin form for 2 hours a week. When I first started, I looked like the monster of Dr. Frankenstein having an upright seizure in the back of the dance studio. The reason I ever started going was due to the quadruple bypass surgery I had at the age of 43. It was a complete surprise to everyone that my heart would be in jeopardy. I worked out 5 days a week and looked physically in better shape than I had ever looked. My workouts were primarily weight lifting. I have never been a fan of cardio. Not because I disagreed with their results but because I tend to have shin splints that burn my legs like a nest of fire-ants being released on infant baby skin. Running was painful, so I just avoided it. I thought working out on my legs was sufficient to keep my insides working in a healthy manner. I was wrong. As it turns out, I needed some cardio to pump that blood through my system in a more active way. After the surgery, the cardiologist encouraged me to get back in the gym but add an element of cardio. Since my last workout program found me with my chest split in half and a doctor holding my heart in his hand, I thought it best to take heed. At first, I tried the treadmill, or should I say, the dread-mill (sorry, I'm not above hack material). It hurt so bad. That's when I remembered all those late sleepless nights in hotels throughout the years. My usual is to keep the tv on so there is background noise happening…perhaps that is why I couldn't sleep. Every time I would wake up past 3am, there would be a Zumba DVD info-mercial on. As an old break dancer, I always thought, that looks fun. So, when walking to the men's restroom in the gym (away from the dread mill), I saw a room full of people dancing to a Pit Bull song, I poked my head in. The instructor invited me in, I watched the feet then decided, I'm gonna try! And try I did. It seemed like it took forever to get my dancing legs back. I know this may sound weird, but I used to LOVE to dance. It may be the Latino blood, whatever it was, I was found every weekend as an upper teenager at a dance-club. I was very frustrated that it took me so long to get the rust off my moves. I would be in the back of the class so focused on getting it right. It was hard, but I committed to go and truth be told, burning 1000 calories in an hour dancing was way better than standing beside a treadmill that I pretended to have just gotten off. As time went by, I found myself moving to the next row up. This was a huge step for me. The last thing I wanted was for anyone to see me messing up the moves. And now, there is a row of Zumba-ers…Zumbees.. behind me. If I screw it up, they all see. I determined, "I am not a back-row person. I am a Tindall, and Tindall's lead. We are the example NOT the exception.". This is something I teach my kids and I had to abide by the same principle, even if (especially if) they aren't around. Because your character is who you are when no one you know is watching. I took on the second row. I may not have been perfect in all the moves, but I was positioned to be present no matter what. Then, one day, it happened. Being a few minutes late for class, I walked in and the only open spot was on the front row. Crap. I was not ready for the pressure that comes along with the front row, but it didn't matter. I was there and if I wanted to take part, I had to go where the opening was. As I stepped into position and started to do the choreography, I investigated the mirror at my reflection, I thought about how in the recent past, I had been laid up in hospital beds, hooked to breathing machines, legs swollen with internal bleeding and unable to get myself out of bed without a physical therapist involved. A smile started to show on my face. Each step had me exuding more and more of the internal joy I contained. I realized just how far I had come and it was a celebration. I was and am a happy man. But beyond the first glace at my smiling face, I focused on the faces behind me. I noticed that none of them where looking at their own reflections, rather, they were focused on my feet. I, the monster of Dr. Frankenstein, was their leader. Something happened in me at that moment, I became the leader they needed me to be. I have always taught that you can't give what you don't have, and that is true, but could it be that we have more than we assume? I would've never just signed up to be a leader in the Zumba world, yet, over time, I was being conditioned to lead. I may not be perfect, but the time I have spent in the back and middle of the class made me a capable leader to those with less time invested. This, I believe is the case with most of us when it comes to tapping into having a passion and zeal for God's kingdom. We go from committing to be present to learning how it works, then, it is our responsibility to take on the role of leading those not yet at our level. The best thing you can do to call yourself into an accountable position is to give what you have to those not yet there. Assume the position of a leader. That front row (and I am not talking about the front row of your church, but if that is part of it for you, then go for it) will cause you to stir yourself up in a way that the back row will never require. Determine that you are a leader, and, in your life, leaders are the example, not the exception. You may be an example of an involved person by being present in the back, but you will not be an example of a leader by never taking the lead. It is time to take the lead. If you want to break the common mindset limitation of having a lack of zeal for God's kingdom, then it's time to move forward and dance. You don't have to be perfect, you just must be willing to fill in the gap that is empty and available. You will look up and reflect on how far you have come. It will put a smile on your face and then you will see the help you are being to others watching your steps. That will push you to a greater level because it holds you accountable. You will now grow, not only for your sake, but, for THEIR sake. Serve and Lead. These investments will be the things that take you from limitation to having a passionate zeal.

Chapter 7 – YESTERDAY

I killed a 3-month old cat. There, I said it. I am not proud of this moment in my life, but I must admit when things are true, and this, my friends, is true. Before you put this book down and call the authorities, let me explain the story. It was not on purpose. I am an animal lover and would never hurt one on purpose. In fact, to the dismay of many of my followers, I have never even been hunting. Yes, it's true, when the deer over populate the earth as is warned by all my hunting friends, it will be my fault. I refused to do my part in killing this vicious, violent animal that terrorizes our streets. I just can't. Don't get me wrong, I will gladly partake of any deer jerky or chili offered. I am just not the guy to be pulling triggers, that is what my wife is for. I'm the earth loving, tree hugging hippie in the house. So, when I say, I killed a cat, you must understand, this was by accident. But, if you asked the cat, it wouldn't matter, dead is dead and this cat is dead. Get your coffee ready, because here comes the story.

Back in 2003, My cat, Spitter, bore unto us, kittens. Spitter (The name given based on her habit of spitting at me when she was young. I'm an adjective guy, I name animals by the adjective that describes them best. I've had animals named such things as Long, Black and White, Round, The Boy dog and the Girl dog. Just whatever stands out as the primary description, that shall be the name. Now back to the story), was not of noble bloodline. More of an alley cat than a palace pet. In my upbringing, I was never exposed to the current, popular notion people abide by today, of not allowing animals to be outside pets. In fact, if you couldn't survive outside, you just ceased to survive. I figure, its God's intent to have creatures be how they were created to be, outside. That being said, I have always allowed them to come in and lounge, as long as we have a mutual understanding that, inside is for the people, and outside is for the animals. No sitting in another spot because a cat or dog is in my chair. Nope, just move the animal. That's the way Jesus did it when He first came here to America with unregistered shotgun in hand and that is good enough for me (Not sure of accuracy of last sentence). I know, even as I write this, I am dealing with 2 different types of judgment right now from the readers. 1, The people who resent me for assuming that a cat is meant to be able to survive outside, and 2, the people who hate cats and can't believe that I would be a cat person. Well let me say this, I love cats. I love dogs equally as much but for different reasons. The thing I respect about cats is their ability and willingness to kill anything within its same size frame and eat it. It confuses me that most men, who try to act real manly, do that thing where they say they hate cats. It doesn't make sense to me. They love UFC, they love boxing, they love most anything that is built for fighting, yet the most stealth species on earth – the feline – gets no respect. Cats are killing machines. Dogs, though I love them, are high-maintainence and needy. They have to get petted to ensure that you love them. They have to be fed to survive. Not cats. You can leave town for 3 weeks and when you get back, a cat will literally be fatter then when you left. They tolerate being pet. I respect that. I am not a fan of needy relationships, therefore, me and cats get along just fine. So when Spitter had these kittens, there was a household understanding among all members that these little jokers would not be inside for very long. They were moved all together into the garage and I kept the bay door slightly opened at the bottom to allow them to start venturing outside. All of them were doing great with the exception of one. This was the runt of the litter. Spitter had done that horrible thing that animals sometimes do where they push the least likely to live to the side and let it fend for itself. Nature can be brutal and this is what is known as Survival of the Fittest. It was kinda the way things worked before Instagram, look it up. Well, I, being an animal lover, could not just watch while this tiny kitten starved to death. I took matters into my own hands and found a tiny syringe and some pet formula at the local pet-store. Everyday I hand fed this little guy, for 8 weeks. Over time, the kittens all gravitated to various places to play. This kittens favorite spot was at the base of my front, drivers side wheel in the driveway. Knowing this, I had a ritual that I would perform every morning before I drove off to work. I would, 1, tap the front grill of my truck (Toyota 4-Runner, for those keeping tabs on the details and texture of the content). This would make a "Thud" sound and alert the kitten to get out from under the truck. 2, I would turn the corner and kick the front tire. Once again, to make the kitten aware that action was taking place. This made a "Thump" sound. And finally, 3, I would honk the horn as a last resort and warning. This, obviously made a "Honk", noise. Usually the kitten would run out upon hearing the initial "Thud". Sometimes he waited for the "Thump" and on very rare occasion, he would hold strong and in place until the "Honk". Nevertheless, the kitten knew to get out of there. Every single day, for 8 weeks, Thud, Thump and Honk. Thud. Thump. Honk. Without hesitation or variation, Thud, Thump, Honk. It was a pattern I had created to guard the relationship I had built over time. This tiny little kitten was still here, as a result of my caring for and nurturing it. Thud, Thump and Honk was no stranger to our morning ritual. 8 WEEKS. THUD, THUMP, HONK. Until one day… - *This is your chance to bail out on this story* –

I was running late for work. It was one of those mornings where the alarm doesn't go off because you somehow pressed pm instead of am. The toaster burned the toast, the iron singed your shirt, the toilet paper is on its last, stuck to the cardboard tube layer. Just everything that could go, did. As I dashed out my front door, I quickly made my way around the truck, turned the corner, opened the door and turned the key. I didn't, Thud. I didn't Thump. And I didn't, Honk. I just ran around the truck, got in and started it up. I backed out of my driveway, turned the wheel, put it in drive and drove forward. About 50 yards later, I felt a slight bump. Followed by a secondary bump. I thought to myself, "hmm, I didn't see any potholes, I wonder what that was". As I slowed down to look in the review mirror, what I saw immediately made me bring the truck to a screeching halt. What I saw was the flattest version of that poor little cat that I had ever seen. It was just laying there. You know how they say cats have 9 lives, well, that isn't the case. 2 lives at best, front wheel and back wheel. At least that seems to be the case with kittens, specifically this kitten. His grey and white coat now covered by tire tread. I sat sickened. Just looking into the mirror as if I could make something magical happen by gazing on the reflection of this horrible scene that had just taken place. I did what any good Christian would do, I prayed for the kitten. I was believing for a miracle to take place. I think I even took up a special miracle offering like they do during pledge season on Christian television, but nay. The kitten just laid their flat. A feeling of physical illness was setting upon me. I couldn't believe it. My mind was rushing with thoughts of regret. All I had to do was, "Thud, Thump and Honk", I told myself. But that information was no longer helpful. The damage was done…the kitten was dead. I killed a 3-month old kitten. The very relationship I had been keeping alive, taking care of and nurturing, was no damaged because of me. I can't tell you how much disgust I felt as I sat there in my truck looking at what was behind me. I stayed still for about 3 minutes. Thinking, regretting, contemplating. After that time, I had to decide what my next step would be. I looked forward, re-started the truck, put it in drive and dove on to work. At this point I can tell that my last statement was not received very well by some of my fellow animal lovers. How could I? How dare I? I know I know, I get it. It seems harsh. For me to just leave the dead kitten there on the road was quite a statement. I didn't mean for it to come across as uncaring, because, I care. I promise. Stop with that look on your face about me driving off. Let me ask you a question oh bleeding hearts of the world. If you were to run into me at a grocery store, well, heck, lets change that to a Lamborghini dealership (If we are gonna just fantasize, we may as well put ourselves in a dream setting), then, as we greet each other, you notice that I am holding in one hand, a dead cat. You would, at minimum, question in your head, "I wonder what the deal is with Elijah carrying around a dead cat". Then, as I explained to you the story I just shared, the thought would arise, "It is weird that you went back and got that cat. Even weirder that you still carry it around with you." It has been years since that day. I could reply excuses like, "but it was my fault", and, "I knew to do better but I didn't, so now, I can't let it go. It was my fault." While these excuses may be valid, they do not justify me taking upon myself the constant presence of a dead cat. There is a time that we need to move forward from the things in our past, even if they were our fault. Me carrying around a dead cat does not make sense. The more the dead cat of my past is brought into my current and future, the weirder it is for others around me. This is the mentality of Yesterday. It demands that we either stay stuck in our past or we bring the past into our present. This will greatly limit our ability to succeed in life. Potential relationships will disengage once they see the dead cat constantly being carried around with us. In a literal sense this sounds silly and obvious, but in the realm of the unseen, we treat this issue very differently. If I could look into the spiritual, mental and emotional areas of your life, I wonder how many dead cats I would see. Issues of the past that we refused to allow ourselves to move forward from. Things that we continue to bring with us into the present. We must make a hard decision to put the vehicle in drive and go to work. I am not saying that we don't do what we can to bring resolve to the situations that we may have caused hurt and pain to others. We do what we can. We offer a genuine apology followed by an example of behavioral change. Even if rejected, this, over time will speak volumes of the type of person you chose to become after learning the lesson that comes along with hurting others. We may never get the forgiveness from others, this is something beyond our control. What we do have is the responsibility to do our part by acknowledging and apologizing. Beyond that, we muar let ourselves off the hook and move forward. If not, shame will set in. Once shame takes root, it controls our minds. We become more and more insecure and forever feel a sense of disqualification. We will never assume that we can have health in certain areas because we have an evidence of dead cats in that same area. There is a big difference between shame and guilt. We may be guilty, but we do not have to walk in shame over the guilt. My great friend, Pastor Drew Isaacs taught me years ago, Guilt states, "I have made a mistake". Shame states, "I am a mistake". Peter and Judas both betrayed Jesus around the same time. Their outcome was very different. While Peter's denial of Christ was no better than Judas' taking a bribe to reveal where Jesus and the boys were hanging out, Peter ended up becoming what Jesus termed as the foundation of the church. Judas, on the other hand committed suicide and his insides spilled out onto the ground below. This had nothing to do with God accepting one and rejecting the other. It was a result of the mindset each embraced. Both knew they did wrong and were guilty, but Judas allowed his guilt to open the door to shame. Shame is the tool the enemy uses to destroy the potential of your future by constantly reminding you of the dead cat moments in your past. Guilt brought Peter to repentance while shame brought Judas to his death. God's intent is for you to do what you can and move forward. Go to work. Going back and picking up the dead cat doesn't help anyone. You must do all you can to acknowledge your wrong and once you do, move forward. If people forgive you or not, that's fine. God forgives you and He wants you to forgive yourself. The shame of the dead cat is over.

Philippians 3:14 – Brethren, I do not count myself to have apprehended it: but one thing I do, forgetting those things which are behind and reaching forward to those things which are ahead, I press toward the goal for the prize of the upward call of God in Christ Jesus.

STEPS IN PRESSING FORWARD:

1. The first thing we must do to break the Yesterday mindset, is to **forgive ourselves** for the dead cats.

2. **Forgive others** that have hurt you.
There have been thousands of messages on this subject over time. What could I say that would reach beyond those? Who am I to assume that my words would be embraced where others have not? I don't know the correct answers to these questions but I do know, that for whatever reason, you are holding this book and reading this chapter. And because of that, it is my responsibility and privilege to walk you through this.

First, let me begin by saying, I do not know what you have been through and the pain you feel is most likely very real. The reasons you have to hold anger toward that person is also, most likely justified. That being said, how is it working out for you so far? The anger you hold toward them may have been helpful to put and keep a safe distance, but has it proven effective in living with a peaceful spirit? Do you find yourself still bringing their name up as the reason things are not working out for you? If so, as much as you don't like them, the reality is, you are still depending on them. You depend on them to be the hurdle every time you engage in an opportunity to move forward. When you stumble, you bring them back into the picture so that you can have a reason to fail. They are not even present, yet you are relying on them as if they are a constant arch enemy. In my work with thousands of people over the past 25 years, I have found that most people are waiting on an apology from the person who hurt them. And yes, I did instruct you to do your part to make things right in the last point, it is not safe to require other to do the same. It would be great if they did, but, friend, what if they don't? Will you live your entire life on a leash bound by your own expectation to receive a heart-felt apology? I think it is safe to assume the person who hurt you will never reach out to make things right. Once you do that, you release both them, and yourself from this leash. They will no longer be tied to you because you do not require anything from them. Assume they will never make things right and choose to forgive them anyway. That will be a powerful moment in your life. You will almost immediately feel a weight lift from your shoulders. Your view on things will shift into a clearer perspective. The reason is, the lens through which you look at life will be changed. Back in the late 90's people started wearing these yellow lens glasses. They looked pretty cool, so I went to the store and purchased a pair. I wore them for a day. When I went home and took them off, I noticed that everything still looked yellowish. It took me about 24 hours before my eyes adjusted back to normal. I never again wore those silly glasses because I didn't want my perspective to be distorted. That is exactly what is happening when we hold on to unforgiveness toward a person. It places a lens over the way we see things. It distorts our perspective. As we remove the lens of unforgiveness, our eyes begin to readjust to reality. As a person filled with the Spirit of God, a sense of peace will once again be the filter that we look at life through.

When I say "forgive", I do not mean you have to re-engage with them, trust them or forget what has been done. The greatest kind of forgiveness is the kind that has full knowledge of the wrong and chooses to extend grace and mercy in the face of it. Jesus knew that the people shouted, "crucify him", yet, he chose to tell the Father, "forgive them, for they know not what they do". His perspective was higher than the initial act of rejection or abuse. He understood exactly what he said, they know not what they are doing. The person who hurt you may have had an understanding on what they were doing in the moments they hurt and betrayed you, but, just like the people present at Jesus' crucifixion, they were clueless about the bigger picture. Just as you were not fully aware of the hurt your actions or words would bring the people you have in your past, neither did they. We all love a testimony of grace and redemption until it comes to the person who wronged us. I have also seen that the enemy (the devil) looks for opportunities to take us down in the same areas we criticize about others. He loves it when Christians look like idiots and hypocrites. In the same measure you judge, you shall be judged. I don't know about you, but I don't want to be held to the short leash I have held others to. If I want grace, I must extend grace. Even when they don't deserve it. Why?

Because if it's a matter of getting justice, then we would all be disqualified. The same way we believe that our sin was a mistake and not our identity, we must allow ourselves to see them in the same way. It may not feel good and you may have to just do it as a step of faith at first but start to declare that you release them from their actions toward you and speak blessings over them. It doesn't have to be to them, but you will find that as you do this in private, your words will change over time in public. It's not an explanation of the End Times or the book of Revelation, but if you follow this advice, it will open your mindset to a new level and allow you the opportunity to succeed. Try it. What you've been doing isn't working...just ask your close friends.

3. Stop looking back
    If I were to get into a car, place a windshield sunscreen on the front window (Not a small one, I'm talking about one of those silvery material from the 70's, full windshield cover), adjust the rearview mirror, turn the key, put the car in drive and start moving forward. Slowly I roll frontwards but the whole time, I never stop looking in my rearview mirror. Chances are, you would ask me to stop because you know what is going to eventually happen. I will end up wrecking the car. When (not if) I do, let's say it causes damage. It doesn't total the car, just busts the headlight and dents the front bumper. As I look over the damage, I complain how I can't seem to do anything without ruining something.

I take a broom, sweep the glass into a pile on the side of the road, get back in the car and once again, continue to move forward…but never take the blinder off the front window. In fact, for whatever crazy reason, I put my focus on my rearview mirror, AGAIN. As I roll in a forward motion, my eyes catch a glimpse of the pile of glass rubbish that had just occurred. I start to reminisce about the good ole days when I used to have both headlights. Frustration begins to stir from within my spirit. "How could God allow this to happen", I ask myself. My eyes will not be taken off this mirror all the while, I must be okay because I am moving forward, right? Nope. You and I both know how foolish it is to move forward while 1, being blinded to what is in front of us, and 2, to only reflect on what is behind us. Eventually, we will find ourselves in the same position over and over. Wrecked. Over time, it will become impossible to move forward because the damage has been too much. That blinder is what we discussed in point 2, unforgiveness. If you determined to forgive, you have removed the blinder from the front windshield. Your potential to see what is in front of you is now open. That is the first part, but, secondly, we have to reprogram ourselves to **not** focus on the past. It seems simple and obvious that someone would get in the car and not obsess with what is behind them (unless you are on a tv show in which you notice that there has been a suspicious car sitting outside your house all day and now you see that same car three vehicles behind you. That's when you utter to your partner, "I think we have company" and pull a hard right into the alley way. Other than that, look forward). Paul said, "Forgetting those things that are behind". He knew that if you focus on what is behind you, you will find yourself repeating the past that created those wrecks over and over. Wreck after wreck, damage after damage. It will keep you from healthily moving forward. And that is the question. If you are moving forward, are you moving forward in a healthy way? Have you 1, removed the blinder of unforgiveness (both of yourself and others), and 2, are you still looking back.

This Yesterday mindset will hold you back. Success is impossible to achieve when you are bound to failure.

When I was in my late teens, there was a beautiful song by Boys to Men titled, It's so hard to say goodbye to yesterday. Man, I loved that song. Those guys can sing. Me and one of my best buddies, Johnny Jackson, would sing our hearts out to that song while ironing our Z Cavariccies and Fresh Prince style rayon shirts as we got ready to go to "the club". It was such a great song, BUT, it would seem that we (society, not just me and Johnny Jackson) have taken on the message as a mentality. We have concluded that since it is so hard to say goodbye to yesterday, we just won't. We will continue to look at it, be saddened by it and complain that our lives are full of nothing but damage. We try to move forward but still end up in ditches. Friend, it's time to take your eyes off the past and look into your potential future. I am not saying you deny the past happened but there is a reason that the front window is much larger than the rearview mirror. It is so you can see what is behind you but focus on what is in front.

I hope this chapter helps you to identify the blinders of unforgiveness in life so that you can remove them. After that, you need to commit to looking forward. Forward movement is not good enough when you keep looking back. You may need assistance in doing so, that is very normal. We only know what we know, so if you do not know how to stop looking back, reach out to a spiritual leader that can help walk you through until you have it down on your own. If you do not have a spiritual leader in your life, reach out to me. I have relationships with awesome pastors and spiritual leaders all over this world, I can connect the dots and get you out of this ditch. Now, if you will excuse me, I have some Z Cavariccies to find online. Also, I wonder where I can get a fresh fade for this hair...

What will you do?

This information has been straight forward and simple.
The New you will require you to fight these 5 mindsets:
CAN'T
REJECTION (fear of)
ATTITUDE (poor)
ZEAL (lack of)
YESTERDAY

These CRAZY thoughts will cause you to be the Screw You that destroys your life. The question now, what will you do? Like all things, this is your choice. You do not have to adhere to any of the points given in this book. You can go on with a Can't mentality, living a can't life. You can be consumed by what others think about you while having a horrible attitude and outlook on life. You can avoid ever being Zealous about the Kingdom of God and His perspective. And you can commit to living your life bound to yesterday's hurts, failures and even successes. If that has been working for you, then, by all means, carry on. But if not, I ask you to apply the information given in this book. Commit to it for 60 days. After that, if you do not see changes and signs of growth, disregard it and move on. My goal is to help you not to hinder you.

Forward movement in a positive direction is what I am after with this. I believe help and deliverance have found their way to your ears and eyes through some of the points made. The question yet remains, What will you do?

The End-*ish*

For addition information on booking Elijah Tindall or other products, go to elijahtindall.com

Made in the USA
Middletown, DE
04 March 2020